Eyes from the Outside

American Society of Missiology Monograph Series

Series Editor, James R. Krabill

THE ASM MONOGRAPH SERIES provides a forum for publishing quality dissertations and studies in the field of missiology. Collaborating with Pickwick Publications—a division of Wipf and Stock Publishers of Eugene, Oregon—the American Society of Missiology selects high quality dissertations and other monographic studies that offer research materials in mission studies for scholars, mission and church leaders, and the academic community at large. The ASM seeks scholarly work for publication in the Series that throws light on issues confronting Christian world mission in its cultural, social, historical, biblical, and theological dimensions.

Missiology is an academic field that brings together scholars whose professional training ranges from doctoral-level preparation in areas such as scripture, history and sociology of religions, anthropology, theology, international relations, interreligious interchange, mission history, inculturation, and church law. The American Society of Missiology, which sponsors this series, is an ecumenical body drawing members from Independent and Ecumenical Protestant, Catholic, Orthodox, and other traditions. Members of the ASM are united by their commitment to reflect on and do scholarly work relating to both mission history and the present-day mission of the church. The ASM Monograph Series aims to publish works of exceptional merit on specialized topics, with particular attention given to work by younger scholars, the dissemination and publication of which is difficult under the economic pressures of standard publishing models.

Persons seeking information about the ASM or the guidelines for having their dissertations considered for publication in the ASM Monograph Series should consult the Society's website—www.asmweb.org.

Members of the ASM Monograph Committee who approved this book are:

Michael A. Rynkiewich, Asbury Theological Seminary (retired)
James R. Krabill, Anabaptist Mennonite Biblical Seminary
Paul V. Kollman, Associate Professor of Theology and Executive Director Center for Social Concerns (CSC), University of Notre Dame

RECENTLY PUBLISHED IN THE ASM MONOGRAPH SERIES

Jonathan S. Barnes, *Power and Partnership: A History of the Protestant Mission Movement*

J. Kevin Livingston, *A Missiology of the Road: Early Perspectives in David Bosch's Theology of Mission and Evangelism*

Eyes from the Outside

Christian Mission in Zones of Violent Conflict

KIM MARIE LAMBERTY

American Society of Missiology
Monograph Series
VOL. 19

PICKWICK *Publications* · Eugene, Oregon

EYES FROM THE OUTSIDE
Christian Mission in Zones of Violent Conflict

American Society of Missiology Monograph Series 19

Pickwick Publications
An Imprint of Wipf and Stock Publishers
199 W. 8th Ave., Suite 3
Eugene, OR 97401

www.wipfandstock.com

ISBN 13: 978-1-62564-199-1

Cataloguing-in-Publication data:

Lamberty, Kim Marie.

Eyes from the outside: Christian mission in zones of violent conflict / Kim Marie Lamberty.

American Society of Missiology Monograph Series 19

x + 158 pp. ; 23 cm. Includes bibliographical references.

ISBN 13: 978-1-62564-199-1

1. Missions—Theory. 2. Missions—Colombia. 3. Violence—Religious aspects. I. Title. II. Series.

BV2854 C7 L23 2014

Books published in the American Society of Missiology Monograph Series are chosen on the basis of their academic quality as responsible contributions to debate and dialogue about issues in mission studies. The opinions expressed in the books are those of the authors and are not represented to be those of the American Society of Missiology or its members.

This book is dedicated to the victims of violence in Colombia: the displaced, the marginalized, the disappeared, and the murdered. It is also dedicated to survivors, who have found ways to sustain their way of life, and to those who accompany them.

Contents

Illustrations

Preface

To be accompanied means that we feel that there are eyes and ears of the international community present in Tiquisio, and eyes and ears of the international community provide a protective shield for Tiquisio.

—Padre Rafael Gallego, Tiquisio, Colombia

During the fall of 2006, I was working in Colombia with Christian Peacemaker Teams, as part of a group of volunteers sent into conflict zones to accompany nonviolent movements, human rights workers, and unarmed communities at risk of violence or displacement. We were invited to escort a group of Colombian lawyers and human rights professionals as they traveled to a remote, violence-ridden zone of the country. Their mission was to assist several communities with their legal petition to the government for an end to the human rights abuses perpetrated on them by the Colombian military and paramilitary forces, which were seen as operating on behalf of the military. The journey to the village that was to be our central meeting place was grueling. We traveled in jeeps through guerrilla-held territory, through places where there had been recent open fighting, on bad roads, and in thick forest. We were stopped at a Colombian Army checkpoint and detained for several hours. They let us go just as dusk fell, making our trip even more dangerous.

We finally neared our destination in the dark of night. As we drove onto the road approaching the first community, about five thousand people were waiting for us. We were told they had been waiting for most of the day. They lined the road, applauding wildly and beating sticks together to make more noise, and accompanied us into their village. I cannot recount this story without being overwhelmed by emotion. I felt that our presence alone meant so much to them, because they knew that they were no longer isolated in their struggle. No longer alone, they found the courage to fight for their rights, and not just in any kind of way. They found the courage to fight for their rights nonviolently, through dialogue and through the legal system.

Acknowledgments

I OFFER MY PROFOUND thanks to the members of the Christian Peacemaker Teams Colombia team. They encouraged this project from the beginning and gave me the space to do the work. I especially want to thank Sandra Milena Rincon and Julian Gutierrez. They both made introductions and arranged interviews with key leaders, and Julian was especially helpful in identifying which communities to study. Without their assistance, this book would not have been possible.

I am grateful to all of my colleagues, friends, and mentors at Catholic Theological Union. In particular, I want to single out Steve Bevans, who was my doctoral thesis advisor and mentor. His work provides a starting point for much of the thinking in this book. I also want to thank Ed Foley and Bob Schreiter, for believing in me and in my work.

Dawn Stover, my oldest and dearest friend, and a professional journalist and editor, did a final edit of the manuscript and created a much-improved experience for the reader. I am deeply grateful for her friendship and for her professional eye.

I am also grateful to Phil Laubner, a colleague at Catholic Relief Services, who took my amateur photos and turned them into something usable for this book.

Lastly, and most importantly, I am grateful to the people of Micoahumado and Tiquisio, who opened their homes and hearts to me. Their stories deserve to be told, and I hope this book does them justice.

In Solidarity,

Kim Lamberty
November 2013

Introduction

DESPITE THE CONSIDERABLE EFFORTS of conflict resolution professionals, peacekeeping forces, and diplomacy, violent conflicts persist. Although the number of large-scale wars appears to be down from its all-time high in the 1980s, smaller conflicts among armed groups, or involving an armed group threatening an unarmed group, continue to proliferate in many parts of the globe. Most of these conflicts are internal, rather than international, and many involve competition over control of natural resources. In response to the escalating numbers of civilian, unarmed victims, in recent decades a number of faith-based organizations and secular human rights organizations have developed international protective accompaniment projects as a means to reduce the scale of violence and protect unarmed actors in zones of conflict.

International protective accompaniment is the placement of nonviolent teams of trained outsiders, backed up by an international support network, into an unarmed community at risk of human rights violations, violence and/or displacement by armed groups. International protective accompaniment is also frequently referred to as human rights accompaniment, peace teams, or simply protective accompaniment. In this study, those terms will be used interchangeably. Secular human rights groups see accompaniment principally as humanitarian work, while faith-based groups understand it as a vocation to peacemaking derived from their relationship with God, their understanding of God's vision for humanity, and their belief that they have a role in realizing that vision.

FOCUS OF THIS INVESTIGATION

This investigation will look at international protective accompaniment as an example of, and a model for, Christian mission in zones of violent

1

conflict. The accompaniers, who are there by invitation, become "eyes from the outside" able to observe and report to the rest of the nation and world. Teams can consist only of members from outside the country, or may comprise a combination of international members and nationals from other regions of the host country. International teams can also work col laboratively with a national or regional organization, such as the Catholic Church, in accompanying a threatened community. In some cases local human rights workers feel threatened, and so they may invite accompani ment from international groups as well.

According to the organizations providing accompaniment, this work lowers the risk of violence and displacement, which often occur because of the perception of impunity—because no one is watching. In lowering the risk, or at least the perception of the risk, accompaniment can also open up space for a community to focus on something other than pure survival. The hope is that it can allow the community to think about economic de velopment, reconciliation, and forging a new future free from violence. One outcome of this investigation will be learning more about the nature of the space that accompaniment opens up.

Groups currently doing international protective accompaniment work include: Peace Brigades International (secular, UK-based), Ecumeni cal Accompaniment Project in Palestine/Israel (World Council of Churches project), Nonviolent Peaceforce (secular, Europe- and US-based), Chris tian Peacemaker Teams (ecumenical, US- and Canada-based), Witness for Peace (Christian, US-based), Operation Dove (Catholic, Italy-based), Michigan Peace Teams (secular, US-based), Presbyterian Accompaniment Project (US-based), and Guatemala Accompaniment Project (religious origins, US-based).

I chose to write on this topic because of my own history working as an accompanier in zones of armed conflict. From 2004 to 2008, I worked in Palestine, Colombia, and Guatemala. In Palestine my team lived in a small village on the West Bank whose inhabitants for many years had been the victims of physical violence, displacement, and land seizure by residents of a nearby Jewish settlement. In Colombia I was part of a team accompa nying communities of subsistence farmers and miners at risk of physical violence, displacement, and land seizure by guerrillas, paramilitaries, and/ or the Colombian Army because of the farmers' proximity to an important natural gas pipeline, and the miners' proximity to valuable mineral depos its. In Guatemala I worked alone for a short period of time accompanying an indigenous village at risk of physical violence, displacement, and land seizure because of their proximity to a large gold mine owned by a Canadian company. From my perspective as an accompanier, it seemed that the presence of outsiders in some cases was a deterrent to violence, and in other cases changed the community's perception of the risk, thereby enabling them to think about something other than pure survival, and to act on behalf of their own future.

But that was my perspective as an accompanier. The question for this investigation will be: What is the perspective of the communities being accompanied? And based on their perception of what accompaniment does for them, is it one possible model for church mission in the twenty-first century? By model I mean that it provides an example for imitation or emulation. If accompaniment is a useful model, then the results of this project could serve as the impetus for church groups to adopt international protective accompaniment as part of their mission work.

This investigation focuses on the perspective of communities being accompanied in order to make explicit the fact that these communities are not merely objects of our accompaniment, or objects of our mission. These communities are not our projects. They are subjects who are artisans of their own destiny and protagonists in their own life projects. This is different than earlier views of Church mission, in which Christianity was often imposed as part of the European conquest. Theologically, the view of the human person as subject of his or her own destiny is based on the principle of Imago Dei found in Genesis 1:26–27: Every human person is created in the image and likeness of God. Recent Catholic Church documents also echo this understanding of Imago Dei. For example, in a Latin American context, the most recent document of the Episcopal Conference of Latin America and the Caribbean (CELAM) states that the pastoral work of human development must ultimately lead to individuals becoming subjects of their own development.[1]

THE LOCATION OF THE INVESTIGATION

The investigation took place in two communities in Colombia, Tiquisio and Micoahumado, which have been profoundly affected by the long-running Colombian civil war. Chapter 1 presents an overview of the history and current situation in Colombia and in these two communities.

Leaders in Tiquisio and Micoahumado first invited accompaniment from a regional group, *Programa de Desarrollo y Paz de Magdalena Medio*

---

1. CELAM, *Documento de Aparecida*, 399.

(Program for Peace and Development in Magdalena Medio, or *Programa* and through *Programa* they requested accompaniment from an international group, Christian Peacemaker Teams.

Programa was formally founded in 2001, although it actually started working in the mid-1990s, in part through the efforts of the Catholic Diocese of Barrancabermeja, and under the guidance of a Jesuit, Father Francisco DeRoux. Padre Francisco served as the first director of *Programa* 2008 he stepped down to become the Provincial of the Colombia Province of the Society of Jesus. In 2012 Padre Francisco received the prestigious Chirac Prize for Conflict Prevention, for his work in the Magdalena Medio region of Colombia—work he began with *Programa*.

Based in Barrancabermeja, *Programa* maintains eight regional offices, including one in the southern part of the Bolivar Department, where Tiquisio and Micoahumado are located. *Programa's* mission involves three different types of overlapping work:

- creating zones of peace and human rights;
- developing local democratic governance through social and cultural processes;
- initiating sustainable and equitable economic development projects.

The goal is integral development that unites the community behind mutually agreed-upon goals that fit under the three areas of work delineated above. The concept of "integral human development," meaning development that is well-rounded, includes all the elements that foster the fullness of life. It was first articulated in the Pope Paul VI encyclical *Populorum Progressio* (On the Development of Peoples), as well as in numerous official Catholic documents since its publication in 1967.[2] The elements of integral human development are political, social, spiritual, economic, cultural, and physical, and *Programa* works to address each of them in its programs.

Programa staff with whom I spoke referred to their work in the communities as "accompaniment." Communities that are accompanied by *Programa* agree to accept principles of social justice, human development, and environmental protection, and to work toward constructing peace in Colombia. Micoahumado was one of *Programa's* first projects; Tiquisio was added a few years later. It was through *Programa's* initiative that local leaders in Micoahumado and Tiquisio invited international protective accompaniment by Christian Peacemaker Teams (CPT). The reasons for

2. Pope Paul VI, *Populorum Progressio*, 14.

inviting CPT and the specific role it has played and continues to play in Micoahumado and Tiquisio are discussed at length in chapter 2.

Christian Peacemaker Teams (CPT) is a Christian organization that places teams of trained volunteers in zones of armed conflict to accompany unarmed communities that are at risk of violence by armed groups. The idea is to reduce the threat of violence and empower communities to act on behalf of their own survival. Christian Peacemaker Teams (CPT) arose from a call during the Mennonite World Conference in 1984 for Christians to devote the same discipline and self-sacrifice to nonviolent peacemaking that armies devote to war. Today, CPT seeks to enlist the whole church in an organized, nonviolent alternative to war. CPT places teams at the invitation of local communities that are confronting situations of lethal conflict. "These teams seek to follow God's spirit as it works through local peacemakers who risk injury and death by waging nonviolent direct action to confront systems of violence and oppression."[3] CPT's roots are in the historic peace churches (Mennonite, Church of the Brethren, and Quaker), and in a biblically based spirituality of nonviolence and respect for human rights.

The call in 1984 came from Ron Sider, founder and president of Evangelicals for Social Action and Professor of Theology at Palmer Theological Seminary. Sider stated:

> Over the past 450 years of martyrdom, immigration and missionary proclamation, the God of shalom has been preparing us Anabaptists for a late twentieth-century rendezvous with history. The next twenty years will be the most dangerous—and perhaps the most vicious and violent—in human history. If we are ready to embrace the cross, God's reconciling people will profoundly impact the course of world history . . . This could be our finest hour. Never has the world needed our message more. Never has it been more open. Now is the time to risk everything for our belief that Jesus is the way to peace. If we still believe it, now is the time to live what we have spoken.[4]

Sider went on to say that Christians must be willing to make the same sacrifices as soldiers, even up to death, if we mean what we say that the "cross is an alternative to the sword."[5] Sider's call sparked vigorous conversations in Anabaptist churches across North America. These discussions

---

3. Christian Peacemaker Teams, "About CPT," http://www.cpt.org/about_cpt.
4. Christian Peacemaker Teams, "History," http://cpt.org/about/history.
5. Ibid.

culminated in a 1986 gathering at a suburban Chicago retreat center owned by the Society of the Divine Word. Out of that gathering a call went out for the formation of Christian Peacemaker Teams (CPT). Although CPT was an initiative of the Anabaptist churches, it is now wholly ecumenical, meaning that it is composed of members of all varieties of Christian faith traditions. Although CPT embraces a Christian identity, CPT works with local partners from other faith traditions.

A noteworthy aspect of Sider's call is that he seems to have under stood it to be a call to "mission," with an understanding of mission as evangelizing, as well as a call to fulfill the Christian churches' mandate to work for peace. For him, evangelizing means showing the world that Jesus is a way to peace. CPT was formed out of this understanding. Although it is rare to hear members of CPT discuss their work as "mission," nearly everyone can quote from Sider's speech, and there is broad understanding of the principles upon which the organization was founded.

INTERNATIONAL ACCOMPANIMENT AS MISSION

This investigation seeks to determine whether the work of CPT, as well as that of other organizations involved in international protective accompa niment, can be grounded within the theology of Christian mission. Based on the most current thinking within Christian missiology, international protective accompaniment appears to be a good fit. International pro tective accompaniment is based in a spirituality of the Cross, where the accompanier takes on the poverty and vulnerability of the accompanied community. In this way, accompaniers are by their very presence witness ing to the Gospel. It is a ministry of presence, friendship, and relationship that requires learning the local language and culture. And it is a ministry that is directed by the needs of the community being accompanied, not by a desire for conquest or power on the part of the missionary. In my experience, most faith-based accompaniment groups do not use mission language in their self-definition because they do not wish to be associated with an old paradigm of Christian mission.

We can compare the nature of international protective accompani ment with what prominent mission theologian Stephen Bevans wrote a few years ago about current trends in missiology:

> We have moved from a missiology of power to a missiology
> of relationship and vulnerability . . . Kosuke Koyama wrote

famously of the need for missionaries today to be converted from a "crusading mind" to a "crucified mind," and in one of his last lectures, entitled "The Vulnerability of Mission," David Bosch focused on Shusaku Endo's powerful novel *Silence*, in which the missionary's identity is not with the powerful . . . but—ultimately—with the crucified Christ . . . What this means in concrete is that being in mission is about sharing deeply in people's lives: building real relationships and friendships with those we serve . . . if necessary sharing their poverty and their own vulnerability, undergoing the self-emptying of learning others' language and culture.[6]

As we will see in chapter 3, Christian mission today is changing. We now look for ways of practicing mission that are grounded in a spirituality based on the vulnerability of the crucified Christ, and thus the need for a mission presence based on relationship, and on living with the community in such a way that the missionary shares in the community's poverty and vulnerability. This is exactly what CPT does.

INTERNATIONAL ACCOMPANIMENT AS PEACEBUILDING

Peacebuilding is another emerging discipline in the twenty-first century. This investigation will examine international accompaniment in light of this discipline in order to determine whether, in addition to providing a model for mission, accompaniment might also be a way of practicing peacebuilding.

Like international accompaniment, peacebuilding as a theology, and as a praxis, evolved in response to the protracted, internal conflicts that marked the twentieth century and continue to this day. Peacebuilding seeks to understand the myriad of factors that contribute to a conflict and to seek solutions based on that understanding. As one scholar describes it:

Peacebuilders strive to address all phases of these protracted conflicts, in which pre-violence, violence, and post-violence periods are difficult to differentiate. Accordingly, peacebuilding engages all sectors of society and all the relevant partners— people living in the local communities who perpetrate the violence or who are directly victimized by it; national elites in the government, business, education, religion, and other sectors;

6. Bevans, "From Edinburgh to Edinburgh," 5–6.

and diplomats, policymakers, scholars, international lawyers, religious leaders, and other professionals who often operate at a geographical distance from the conflict.[7]

Furthermore, the focus is not on whether use of force is an appropriate or ethical response to acts of injustice, which is addressed by just-war theory, but on how to help societies devastated by war or unjust regimes to heal and to build a just social order without resorting to further violence. Using this definition, international accompaniment would seem to be part of a peacebuilding praxis that addresses conflict at the level of communities affected by violence.

The Catholic Peacebuilding Network (CPN) is an organization of Catholic theologians, practitioners, educational institutions, organiza tions, and individuals formed in 2004 and devoted to building peace. CPN held a groundbreaking conference on peacebuilding at the University of Notre Dame in April 2008. This conference, the first of its kind, brought together prominent Catholic theologians and social scientists, and Catho lic practitioners of peacebuilding. Throughout the conference, themes of accompaniment and solidarity were prominent. In a plenary presentation that I attended, Mgsr. Hector Fabio Henao, national director of Catholic Social Action (*Pastoral Social*) in Colombia, defined accompaniment as walking with, and placing oneself in the situation of, those who suffer atrocities directly. He also stressed the need to offer a methodology of accompaniment. However, the conference did not offer a concrete dis cussion of the praxis of international protective accompaniment. What does international accompaniment do? Is it effective? And if so, how is it effective?

The results of this case study will answer those questions, and add to current Catholic thinking about peacebuilding. It will bring together mission and peacebuilding praxis. In other words, it will develop a mis sion praxis of international protective accompaniment that is also a peace building praxis.

METHODOLOGY

This investigation is a work of practical theology. It seeks to analyze a given context, reflect on it in light of Christian tradition and theology, as well as the lived experience of the minister or ministers working in that

---

7. Appleby, *Peacebuilding and Catholicism*, 3.

context, and develop an appropriate pastoral response. A variety of authors have developed methods by which this process is accomplished. I believe that the quality of the results depends on the quality of the method. Because we are seeking a praxis that places conflict-ridden communities as subjects and protagonists in their own future, the methodology for this investigation begins with the experience of the communities. Thus, this investigation uses an adapted version of the *pastoral circle* method found in Peter Henriot and Joseph Holland's 1984 book, *Social Analysis*. The method begins with *insertion* into a given situation, moves to *social analysis, theological reflection*, and *pastoral response.*

Insertion means looking specifically at the Colombia context, where the case study will take place. Chapter 1 provides a brief overview of Colombia and the factors that have led to the seemingly intractable civil war there. Chapter 2 listens directly to the voices of Colombians affected by the violence. The operating assumption in starting with *insertion* is that we cannot develop an appropriate Christian mission project without a thorough understanding of the context in which we are placing ourselves.

Social analysis involves understanding the insertion experience in all its interrelationships. It "examines causes, probes consequences, delineates linkages, and identifies actors."[8] In other words, the overview of the Colombia context does not just provide a description. It also attempts to identify the root causes of violence, violations, and displacement in Colombia. The assumption here is that an appropriate pastoral response addresses root causes. Thus, this project involves social analysis at every level, woven throughout. I will pay particular attention to the social analysis that the communities themselves are engaging in, because these communities hold the greatest understanding of their own situation, and based on it they have developed their own conclusions about the benefits of international accompaniment.

Theological reflection involves an effort to understand international protective accompaniment in light of faith and church tradition. Theological reflection assesses the results of the case study, together with social analysis, in light of current trends in missiology and peacebuilding. This is an effort to see whether and how international protective accompaniment falls within the Christian tradition as articulated by current thinking in theology.

Pastoral planning asks what *pastoral response* is called for as a result of the first three movements of the circle. Chapter 4 offers both

---

8. Holland and Henriot, *Social Analysis*, 8.

commendations and recommendations regarding the praxis of interna
tional protective accompaniment as practiced by Christian Peacemaker
Teams in Colombia.

The starting point of this project is the voices of those who are affect
ed by accompaniment. The case study took place in Colombia in two com
munities where I have never worked as an accompanier. There are several
important reasons for choosing Colombia. I have worked in Colombia,
speak the language, feel comfortable in the culture, and have colleagues
there who agreed to provide some logistical assistance with the project.
Furthermore, a number of communities in Colombia have had years of ex
perience with accompaniment organizations, including national, regional,
and international actors. Finally, and not least importantly, the conflict in
Colombia contains many of the elements found in most contemporary
conflicts, and as such is a good example to study. R. Scott Appleby, Direc
tor of the Kroc Institute for International Peace Studies at the University
of Notre Dame, names those elements as follows: (1) Conflicts are trans-
boundary, involving local, regional, national, and global actors; (2
involve multiple cultural actors, such as religious, indigenous, colonial,
racial, etc.; (3) they last a long time, and are not easily put to rest; and
(4) the people are involved at all levels, and non-government organiza
tions (NGOs) exercise mammoth influence.[9] Appleby calls the conflict in
Colombia a "perfect storm," in the sense that it is so comprehensive that it
has become an ideal case study for peacebuilders.[10]

Tiquisio and Micoahumado, the locus of this investigation, are two
communities where I have never worked as an accompanier myself but
which have extensive experience with being accompanied. Both com
munities receive short-term international accompaniment (regular visits
by Christian Peacemaker Teams but not permanent presence) along with
more permanent accompaniment by a Colombian group (*Programa*
This is a common form of international protective accompaniment and
allows the international accompaniers to involve themselves in multiple
communities.

The *Aparecida* document of CELAM referenced earlier underscores
the responsibility of the Catholic Church of Latin America to accompany
the poor of Latin America, "even including martyrdom."[11] Catholic pas
toral workers have provided a good deal of accompaniment in conflict

9 Appleby, *Many Dimensions of Catholic Peacebuilding*, 5.

10. Ibid., 1.

11. CELAM, *Documento de Aparecida*, 396.

zones in Colombia, and many have received death threats and therefore have been displaced. One important question this study asked was, from the perspective of the community, which type (or combination of types) of accompaniment is most effective at reducing violence or the threat of violence? This analysis led to a model that takes advantage of the resources of both local churches and international missionaries.

I conducted a total of twenty-one interviews during November and December of 2008. Nineteen interviews were with community leadership in Tiquisio and Micoahumado (seven from Tiquisio and twelve from Micoahumado) and two interviews were from the leadership of *Programa*, CPT's main inviting organization in Colombia. All interviews were recorded on a digital voice recorder. They range in length from ten minutes to several hours.

I am aware of the concern about whether or not people from accompanied communities told me the truth. In the case of Tiquisio, several people whom I interviewed had no information that I was also a member of CPT, but several other people knew me from previous accompaniments in a different context. My experience was that those who knew me as a member of CPT were far more willing to talk openly about their very difficult experiences with armed groups. In general I found that most people were very willing to offer suggestions for improving CPT's work, leading me to believe that they were not feeling constrained by their relationship with the organization.

In the case of Micoahumado, I arrived in the village with a CPT-sponsored international delegation. I did not conduct any interviews while the CPT delegation was present in the community, and only one member of the community leadership actually knew me as a member of CPT from a different context. However, although I did not dress in the CPT uniform or introduce myself as a member of CPT, I think some people made assumptions about my connections with the organization. Further, I found that many people, in both communities, tended to lump all of the international visitors together and did not see that there were differences between the various groups or types of visitors. In those cases, people would offer suggestions by saying "you" should do this or that.

CPT has been accompanying Micoahumado longer than Tiquisio and is very well known there. My sense was that my perceived affiliation with the organization was an asset. CPT has built up an enormous amount of trust over the years with the community, and as a result, I believe that the people I interviewed said things to me that they would not have said to an unaffiliated doctoral student. Their openness with me was a tribute to CPT's work, in my view. They did not seem reticent about offering suggestions for improvement, while at the same time expressed gratitude for CPT's presence. They also gave me copies of documents and trusted me not to misuse them. They told me that they had several experiences with journalists in the past who had misquoted or misunderstood them.

ORGANIZATION OF THE INVESTIGATION

The first chapter of this investigation is an initial insertion into the Colombia context: the history and culture of Colombia as it pertains to this study; an explanation of the conflict, the various armed groups, and the effects it has had on society; and a deeper description of the two communities where the study takes place. Chapter 2 narrates the results of my interviews with community leaders in Tiquisio and Micoahumado.

Chapter 3 takes a deeper look at current trends in mission theology, using the following three texts:

- Bosch, David. *Transforming Mission: Paradigm Shifts in Theology of Mission*. Maryknoll: Orbis, 1991.

- Bevans, Stephen and Schroeder, Roger. *Constants in Context: A Theology of Mission for Today*. Maryknoll: Orbis, 2004.

- Suess, Paulo. *Evangelizar desde los proyectos históricos de los otros* Quito: Abya-Yala, 1995.

Transforming Mission, a survey of Christian mission from its inception to the present day, which culminates in a proposal for an emerging new paradigm in mission, has become a classic text in world mission studies. Any look at trends in missiology would be incomplete without this study. Building on the work of Bosch, the book by Bevans and Schroeder proposes a contemporary theology of mission in light of historical trends. Paulo Suess, one of the most respected Latin American missiologists, writes about the importance of doing mission work that responds to the life projects of the receiving communities. A survey of all three books, along with some supplementary material, provides the reader with a solid grounding in the current state of the theology of Christian mission.

Chapter 4 considers the results of the case study in chapter 2 in light of the conclusions about theology of mission in chapter 3. Chapter considers and brings into the dialogue my experience and the experience of CPT as practitioners of international accompaniment. The analysis places international protective accompaniment within the theology of mission as articulated in chapter 3. In doing so, chapter 4 articulates a theology and praxis of Christian mission in zones of violent conflict.

Chapter 5 briefly describes current thinking about Catholic peacebuilding, which emphasizes the theological themes of accompaniment and solidarity, based on papers and notes from the Catholic Peacebuilding Conference described earlier, and on the text *Peacebuilding: Catholic Theology, Ethics, and Praxis*, edited by Robert J. Schreiter, R. Scott Appleby, and Gerard F. Powers, 2010. I conclude by proposing international protective accompaniment as one tool for an effective peacebuilding praxis.

GOALS, LIMITATIONS, AND AUDIENCE

The goal of this investigation is to develop a renewed praxis of Christian international protective accompaniment that takes into account the voices of accompanied communities, and that will be useful to both the accompaniment groups and to those who think about how to do mission in the twenty-first century, as well as to those who think about how to do peacebuilding. Its limitations are that it was only possible to do a case study in one country, for the sake of manageability. It would be interesting, for example, to compare the comments of accompanied communities in different parts of the world to see whether their perspectives are the same. Instead, I draw some broad conclusions from one country. Nonetheless, I expect these conclusions to be useful for those who are seeking ways of doing mission that are not hegemonic or colonial, but at the same time genuinely impact the lives of those being served, and respect the freedom and agency of local people. I hope that it serves as a starting point for further reflections on accompaniment.

1

The Colombia Context

THIS CHAPTER PROVIDES AN overview of the factors—historical, cultural, geographical, and religious—that impact, and have impacted, Colombia's long-running internal conflict. Understanding the conflict's actors, as well as its causes, enables the reader to draw conclusions about the role of outside accompaniment later in this investigation. The assumption is that we cannot determine an appropriate role for Christian mission without first understanding the context within which we plan to place the mission. Indeed, while I was conducting the interviews for the case study presented in chapter 2, many Colombians told me that international organizations should not send people to Colombia who do not understand the situation, because they can do more harm than good. Although this overview is brief, the analysis here is needed in order to craft an appropriate response for Christian mission in this zone of violent conflict.

BRIEF SKETCH OF COLOMBIA

Colombia, the fourth largest country in South America, shares borders with Venezuela, Peru, Brazil, Panama and Ecuador, and has coasts on both the Caribbean and the Pacific. It boasts a highly varied geography, including coastal lowlands, mountainous highlands, fertile valleys, plains, rainforest, and more than twenty thousand kilometers of rivers. More than 95 percent of the population resides in the valleys and along the rivers within the western, mountainous, part of the country.

Colombia's largely urban population of more than forty million is estimated to be made up of approximately 58 percent mestizo (mixed

Spanish and indigenous), 20 to 30 percent white, meaning that they iden
tify themselves as fully Spanish or with other European ancestry,
percent Afro-Colombian or mixed African and white or indigenous, and
3.4 percent indigenous peoples.[1] This breakdown is taken from a Library
of Congress profile completed in 2007, but the article makes clear that
the ethnic breakdown is approximate. One finds different percentages in
other publications, especially with respect to the percentage of indigenous
people, which varies from 1 percent to the 3.4 percent found in the Library
of Congress profile, and with respect to the number of people with African
ancestry, which is sometimes estimated at nearly 20 percent. The upper
class, approximately 5 percent of the population, mainly identifies itself as
white, and the middle class, about 20 percent of the population, is mostly
mestizo or white. Thirty-four percent of the population lives below Co
lombia's poverty line, and these are mostly mestizo, indigenous, or Afro-
Colombian, and most of them live in rural areas.[2] About 75 percent of
the population resides in urban areas, largely concentrated in four major
cities: Bogotá, Medellin, Cali, and Barranquilla.[3]

Colombia is traditionally a Roman Catholic country, although the
Constitution of 1991 gives Colombians the right to freely practice other
religions. At least 87 percent of Colombians identify as Roman Catholic,
and estimates go as high as 95 percent.[4] The Catholic Church has played an
extraordinarily active role in working for peace in Colombia at all levels:
local, regional, and national. At a formal level, the Colombian Conference
of Bishops (CEC) has advocated for a negotiated settlement to the conflict
that involves dialogue with all of Colombian society. The CEC itself has
participated in formal dialogues and negotiations, sometimes publicly and
sometimes behind the scenes, for an end to the violence. One Church ac
tivity important for our investigation involves sponsoring what are called
pastoral dialogues. Under Colombian law, only government officials and
Catholic clergy are permitted to negotiate directly with armed actors.
Members of the clergy hold these dialogues locally and regionally and can
thus create the space for encounters between warring factions, or between
armed groups and threatened communities. These dialogues have assisted
threatened communities with removing blockades, eliminating threats

1. Library of Congress Federal Research Division, *Country Profile: Colombia*
2. Ibid., 8, and *CIA World Fact Book: Colombia*, Economy Overview.
3. Library of Congress Federal Research Division, *Country Profile: Colombia*
4. Ibid., 9.

of displacement, and returning kidnapping victims.[5] Pastoral dialogues played an important role in the resolution of Micoahumado's problems with armed groups, which is discussed in detail in the next chapter. Because of their deep involvement in Colombian conflicts, numerous Catholic bishops, priests, and pastoral workers have been threatened, displaced and killed.

Map of Colombia

---

5. Garcia Duran, "Peace Mobilization in Colombia," 13.

HISTORICAL FACTORS IN THE CONFLICT

The roots of the conflict in Colombia are complex, and a complete his tory is beyond the scope of this investigation. In fact, no consensus exists within Colombian society as to the root causes of the violence. There are multiple actors and historical processes at play, a reason for the difficulty in reaching a negotiated solution.[6] Some context, however incomplete, is necessary so that the reader can understand references made in the inter views in chapter 2.

One can find roots of the present-day Colombia conflict in the his tory of Spanish colonization. From the beginning of the sixteenth century, the most isolated and peripheral areas of Colombia were settled by groups marginalized by the Spanish conquerors: mestizos, Afro-Colombians, people of mixed African and other heritage, and poor whites. These most ly subsistence farmers fled to the periphery to escape a situation of land ownership highly concentrated in the hands of the elite in other areas. Tra ditionally, the Colombian state has not been present in these peripheral areas, and control was left to local authorities. These isolated areas were never well integrated into the rest of the Colombian state, and this lack of integration is one factor that has contributed to the present-day conflict. As noted earlier, even today 75 percent of the population is concentrated in just four urban areas.

Even after the end of Spanish rule, in 1810, concentration of rural lands in the hands of a few continued. These large landowners formed part of the governing elite, but remained distant from the people who actually lived on the lands. The *campesinos* living and working on the lands did not hold title to them, leading to a precarious existence and regular violent clashes among groups competing for control of the land.[8]

The current armed conflict can be traced to a period called "La Violencia," a civil war between the two ruling parties, Liberal and Con servative. During the nineteenth and first half of the twentieth century, there were frequent violent clashes between these parties. The violence intensified in the 1940s and 50s, when it spread across the entire coun try, and an estimated 200,000 people were killed. Rural Liberals formed guerilla self-defense groups, and Conservatives countered with their own paramilitary forces, along with hired assassins. The two parties reached a

6. Gonzalez, *Colombian Conflict in Historical Perspective*.

7. Ibid., 11.

8. Ibid.

power-sharing agreement called the National Front that lasted from 1958 to 1974; however, this agreement eliminated any political competition and further isolated the traditionally marginalized groups in Colombia.[9]

> In this context revolutionary guerrilla movements appeared in the 1960s, due as much to the persistence of the campesinos' problems as to the increasing radicalization of university students and the urban middle classes. From this the Cuban-inspired National Liberation Army (ELN) was formed in 1964 by middle-class students and intellectuals, trade unionists and former Liberal guerrilla members. In 1967 the Maoist-influenced Popular Liberation Army (EPL) was created as the armed wing of the Leninist Communist Party. The self-defense groups influenced by the Communist Party in peripheral areas of campesino colonization transformed into the guerrilla group of the Revolutionary Armed Forces of Colombia (FARC) in 1966, after they had been attacked by the Army.[10]

Originally established in order to regulate the relationships between coca-growing campesinos in the peripheral areas of the country, and drug traffickers, by the late 1970s and 1980s the guerrilla forces began to expand and move out of the margins of the country. They began levying taxes on campesino crops, and eventually became involved in drug trafficking themselves. To finance their operations, they began to use kidnapping and extortion, and this partly gave rise to various paramilitary forces, supported by the Colombian elite and also financed by drug trafficking.[11]

During this same period, indigenous groups began organizing, and the National Indigenous Organization of Cauca (ONIC) was formed as a peaceful means to defend against a brutal effort by Colombia's power elite to break up indigenous land reserves that are collectively owned. In 1990 Quintín Lame, an indigenous guerrilla group, demobilized and joined the peaceful political process, a move that helped to facilitate passage of the new Constitution in 1991. Although the 1991 Constitution recognized indigenous rights, according to interviews with indigenous groups, these rights are rarely upheld, and indigenous groups have fallen victim to murder and displacement by paramilitary groups seeking control over their lands.[12]

---

9. Ibid., 12.

10. Ibid., 13.

11. Ibid.

12. Goodner, *Colombia's Bad Indians' Uprising*, para. 16ff.

THE PRESENT-DAY CONFLICT

Colombia's long-running conflict has created a humanitarian crisis. More than four million Colombians have been internally displaced, and it con tinues: more than one hundred thousand are displaced each year. Those with a history of political, social, and economic exclusion have been par ticularly hard hit: 25 percent of those displaced have been identified as Afro-Colombian. In addition, human rights groups, trade union leader ship, indigenous and Afro-Colombian leadership, and leadership within displaced communities face death threats and other abuses. Since twenty-nine hundred trade unionist killings have been documented.

Displacement mostly affects rural campesino, Afro-Colombian, and indigenous communities. With nowhere else to go, they frequently flee to urban areas, where their prospects are dim. They often end up unemployed, with little or no access to health care, decent housing, or education. Many end up in urban settlements, living in substandard conditions.[14] Displaced women and girls are at an elevated risk for gender-based violence, accord ing to government studies.

In addition to displacement, Colombian civilians face violence and threats of violence from all of the armed groups, and this also dispropor tionately affects rural areas. Three main kinds of armed actors have histor ically been involved in the conflict: government security forces, left-wing guerilla groups, and right-wing paramilitaries. The government security forces are the military and the police. The left-wing guerilla movements are largely the Revolutionary Armed Forces of Colombia (FARC) and the National Liberation Army (ELN). Until their demobilization, the right-wing paramilitary forces fell under an umbrella organization called United Self-Defense Forces of Colombia (AUC). While all three factions commit human rights abuses, it is widely recognized that the paramilitary forces have been the worst offenders.

> Paramilitary groups have ravaged much of Colombia for two decades. Purporting to fight the equally brutal guerrillas of the left, they have massacred, tortured, forcibly "disappeared," and sadistically killed countless men, women, and children. Wherever they have gone, they have eliminated anyone who opposed them, including thousands of trade unionists, human rights defenders, community leaders, judges, and ordinary ci vilians. To their enormous profit, they have forced hundreds of

13. Human Rights Watch, *World Report 2013: Colombia*, para. 20.

14. Lari, *Striving for Better Days*, vii.

thousands of small landowners, peasants, Afro-Colombians, and indigenous persons to flee their families' productive lands. The paramilitaries and their supporters have often taken the abandoned lands, leaving the surviving victims to live in squalor on city fringes, and leaving Colombia second only to Sudan as the country with the most internally displaced people in the world.[15]

Many Colombian civilians understand the paramilitary forces as operating on behalf of Colombian government security forces. Indeed, the world was given concrete evidence of this common local belief when the discoveries of army officers' ties to paramilitary groups were published in the international press:

> Ever Veloza, a top paramilitary commander being held in the Itagui prison outside Medellin, said in a recent jailhouse interview that army officers who collaborated with paramilitary units encouraged them to bury the dead or toss their bodies into the river. The victims included trade union members and leftist activists, he said, as well as peasants caught between warring sides. "We would kill people and leave them in the street, and the security forces told us to disappear them . . . ," said Veloza.[16]

Former Colombian President Alvaro Uribe fired high-ranking General Mario Montoya in 2008 over his involvement in the deaths of civilians. A C.I.A. memo obtained in 2008 by *The Los Angeles Times* tied General Montoya to collaborations with paramilitaries.[17] However, in 2011 and 2012, several former paramilitary members charged that Uribe himself had maintained ties to paramilitary groups, a charge that Uribe denies.[18] Furthermore, more than one hundred fifty former and current members of Colombia's Congress have been investigated for paramilitary involvement, and fifty-five have been convicted.[19]

Although former President Uribe conducted a high-profile demilitarization of paramilitary groups that he reported completing in 2006, human rights abuses continue unabated in Colombia. Although more than thirty thousand participated in the demobilization process, many of them were not actually paramilitaries. Paramilitary organizations remained

15 Human Rights Watch, *Breaking the Grip?*, 4.

16. Forero, "Unearthing Secrets of Colombia's Long War," A06.

17. Romero, "Colombian Army Commander Resigns," para. 11.

18. Human Rights Watch, *World Report 2013: Colombia*, para. 13.

19. Ibid., para. 11.

active, sometimes reorganizing under new names but with the same lead
ership. Furthermore, the FARC and ELN continue abuses against civilians
as well, and are known for their use of landmines and other indiscriminate
weapons, and for recruiting and using child soldiers. The Colombian mili
tary continues to commit extrajudicial killings; as of August 2012,
cases were being investigated, involving nearly three thousand victims.
The vast majority of these killings took place between 2004 and 2008
have not been resolved. Although such killings have decreased since
cases were still reported in 2011 and 2012.[20] Furthermore, attacks on hu
man rights defenders are actually on the rise, increasing from 239 attacks
in 2011 to 357 in 2012.[21] In short, evidence indicates that paramilitary
groups have not fully demobilized, that new armed groups are emerging.
Further, in some places where paramilitaries have demobilized, guerrilla
groups are taking over.

Colombia's civilian indigenous, *campesino*, and Afro-Colombian
communities, who have been hardest hit by the violence, consider them
selves to be in a battle over control of their historical lands and of their
own economic development.

> Indigenous CRIC representative Demetrio Moya Obispo said
> the political struggle in Colombia is integrated with the eco-
> nomic struggle against wealthy landowners and multinational
> companies. Because of this, Obispo said, the indigenous strug-
> gle is interrelated with the struggle of *campesinos*, labor unions,
> and Afro-Colombians.[22]

The pattern has been that paramilitary forces seize land that is collectively
owned, or for which the inhabitants do not have a title, forcing the in
habitants to displace. Then the land is turned over to a large landowner
or multinational corporation, which exploits the land for its own profit.
Seized lands are commonly replanted with palm oil—a biodiesel fuel—or
other lucrative cash crops. Recognizing this pattern is important to under
standing the comments of *campesinos* in chapter 2, who say their struggle
is for a new economic model, one which benefits them.

There has also been progress. In 2011 Colombia passed the Victims
and Land Restitution Law, designed to return lands stolen from displaced
persons. As of this writing, implementation has begun but has progressed
very slowly. In addition, In October 2012 peace talks opened between the

20. Ibid., para. 15.

21. US Office on Colombia, "Attacks on Human Rights Defenders," para. 1.

22. Goodner, *Colombia's Bad Indians' Uprising*, para. 26.

Colombian government and FARC, and in May 2013 they reached agreement over the contentious issue of land reform, the first of six points they plan to address in the negotiations. Land tenure has been a major factor in the violence, and this agreement pledges the government to a program of land redistribution and titling, as well as economic and social development in the long-neglected rural areas. It was a major breakthrough and harbinger of hope that an end may finally be in sight. As of this writing, it is too soon to know whether or how the agreement will be implemented, and no implementation will take place unless there is agreement on the remaining negotiating points and a comprehensive peace accord is signed. Furthermore, in August 2013 Colombia was embroiled in a national strike, which started as a rural *campesino* uprising against poverty and the land-use policies of the current government, and has since spread to other labor groups and students. In short, the conflict in Colombia is far from resolved.

THE ROLE OF THE UNITED STATES

The rural victims of this war commonly cite the role of the United States as critical for creating the conditions that enable the conflict to continue. Further, as becomes clear later, understanding the role of the United States holds the key to understanding the function of international accompaniment. As with our discussion of the conflict itself, it is not possible to provide an exhaustive discussion of United States' policy in Colombia. Here I simply present a brief overview so that the reader can understand the issues involved with accompaniment later in this study.

Colombian security forces involved with many of the violations of human rights in Colombia, either through support for paramilitary groups or through extra-judicial killings and other direct abuses, have been funded and/or trained by the United States.

> Another troubling fact is that many alleged extrajudicial executions occur in areas where U.S. assistance has been used to train and equip Colombian security forces. In fact, the regions with the most killings by Colombian security forces in 2006–2007 were essentially the same areas where the military units received significant U.S. assistance. In addition, from 2000–2003, U.S. security assistance to Colombia equaled roughly $1.5 billion, increasing to $2.5 billion from 2004–2007. In the same period, there was a noted increase in executions.[23]

23. US Office on Colombia, *Body Counts & Injustice*, 7.

In 2000, the United States launched an ambitious aid program, known as Plan Colombia, designed to help Colombia combat illicit drugs. Initially, 80 percent of the aid was military, a figure that was reduced in 2006 65 percent. What this means is that the United States has been providing assistance to a military that supports the brutal activities of paramilitary groups in Colombia.

The post-2000 military buildup led to a weakening of Colombia's guerrillas, but not to a decline in human rights abuses or in defense spending. Moreover, nine years later, Colombia's production of cocaine was virtually unchanged,[24] and the production of cocaine fuels all sides of the conflict. Despite more than eight billion dollars in total aid from the United States since 2000, peace in Colombia is still a distant prospect. Al though there have been high-profile victories against FARC, and the war is no longer as visible in Colombia's large metropolitan areas, rural areas still suffer from being on the front lines of armed conflict and cocaine production.

A large and participatory process of gatherings and interviews within Colombian civil society that took place in 2005, through the work of the US Institute of Peace, revealed that Colombian civil society recog nizes that this war will not end by military means; rather, it will end when the economic disparities that divide the country are resolved.[25] Thus, US military assistance serves to further militarize a conflict that will end only through negotiations and economic development.

While Plan Colombia fuels human rights violations, when I was conducting interviews in 2008, Colombia's marginalized groups viewed a proposed US Free Trade Agreement with Colombia as providing further incentives for Colombia's elite to seize rural lands and exploit them for lu crative cash crops. Because of the pattern of paramilitary seizure of lands for economic exploitation by Colombia's elite, Human Rights Watch, in its October 2008 report, recommended that the United States Congress refrain from ratifying a Free Trade Agreement until Colombia shows "concrete and sustained results" in dismantling the paramilitary groups and in holding them, and their political accomplices, accountable for their abuses.[26]

The Obama Administration, over the objections of human rights organizations and labor leaders, signed the Free Trade Agreement with

24. Haugaard et al., *Compass for Colombia Policy*, 27–28.

25. Bouvier, *Harbingers of Hope*, 2–3.

26 Human Rights Watch, *Breaking the Grip?*, 24.

Colombia in 2011. The agreement eliminated tariffs on 80 percent of US exports and will phase out the remainder in future years. The International Trade Commission estimates a $1.1 billion expansion of exports from the United States to Colombia.[27] A 2011 study commissioned by Oxfam International predicted that the agreement would lead to a dramatic decrease in income for Colombia's small farmers—precisely those who have been most affected by the war. Specifically, Oxfam's research revealed that the agreement would result in a decrease in domestic prices for agricultural goods, especially food products, thereby decreasing the incomes of the small farmers who produce them. Small farmers represent 10 percent of the total population of employed people in Colombia. Many of them already live below the official poverty line for Colombia. Although not all of Colombia's products compete with the United States, the report concludes that farmers who do compete will see an overall 16 percent drop in their income.[28] These conclusions are consistent with those of the *campesinos* themselves, who believe the agreement will lead to further displacement. They believe that they will no longer be able to make a living with traditional products, and that their lands will be seized for production of cash crops or other commodities that become even more lucrative under the new agreement. The national strike taking place in August 2013 and referenced earlier, specifically names the Free Trade Agreement as the problem that needs to be addressed.

Because of Plan Colombia and the Free Trade Agreement, Colombia's *campesinos*, and the human rights organizations that support them, believe that the United States holds profound influence over the future of the conflict in Colombia, and therefore over their futures.

27. Norby and Fitzpatrick, "Horrific Cost of the US-Colombia Trade Agreement," para. 7.

28 Garay Salamanca et al., *Impact of the US-Colombia FTA*, 16–21.

The sign reads "Obama: We do not want the Free Trade Agreement."

Thousands of Colombia's indigenous peoples, supported by a variety of labor groups, marched Oct–Dec 2008. There were many reasons given for the march; one was to express opposition to the US Free Trade Agreement. In 2013 they are marching again.

THE MAGDALENA MEDIO REGION

The interviews in the next chapter took place in the Magdalena Medio region of Colombia. The Magdalena Medio region is comprised of four different departments, or states: Santander, Bolivar, Antioquia, and Cesar, and is crossed from north to south by the Magdalena Medio river, the largest river in Colombia. The region covers an area of thirty *municipios*, similar to counties in the United States, with eight hundred thousand inhabitants.

Map Courtesy of Programa de Desarrollo y Paz de Magdalena Medio, www.pdpmm.org. The place names are the names of municipios, separated by the gray-line boundaries.

Magdalena Medio has been battered by the war, mainly because of the region's strategic importance. The region is rich in natural resources, and also lies along the trade route to the Atlantic and to Venezuela. Barrancabermeja, the region's largest city, is home to the country's largest petrochemical refinery. Because of its resources, the region contributes significantly to Colombia's economy, but at the same time in several of its *municipios*, 90 percent of the population do not have their basic needs met. Land is concentrated in the hands of a few, and many *campesinos* not hold titles to the land they live and work on. This struggle over land ownership underlies much of the conflict in the region.[29]

Historically, the Magdalena Medio region was an area of internal colonization by *campesinos* that was not accompanied by a strong state presence, and the absence of the state is still felt today. That void was filled by guerrilla groups from the 1960s until about 1998, when paramili tary groups forcibly took control of the region. It is a context marked by poverty, violence, and social stigmatization due to a perception that the *campesinos* are collaborating with the guerrilla.[30]

The regional organization, *Programa de Desarrollo y Paz de Mag dalena Medio (Programa)* was described in the Introduction. As noted, *Programa* works in the Magdalena Medio region for an integral peace that includes human rights, support for social organizations, and economic development. Started by a Jesuit, Francisco DeRoux, SJ, *Programa* strong credibility within Colombian civil society. *Programa's* is a peace and development process constructed from below, with broad participation by members of the communities it serves. *Programa* supports nearly ninety development and conflict resolution projects in the Magdalena Medio re gion. During the course of its existence, four members of *Programa* been kidnapped, and nine have been killed by paramilitaries.[31]

Programa has a vision for the future of Colombia very different than the past that this region is struggling to recover from.

> It represents a contribution to the transformation of the political culture and toward a future constructed participatively, through promoting opportunities for public and democratic decision-making... It is also an attempt to draw up a new social contract in which the Colombian state will be the guarantor of the general interest, a legitimate structure which regulates conflicts, a valid instrument of social cohesion capable of uniting Colombians, and promoting real economic and social development for all, with emphasis on the poorest.[32]

29. Katz Garcia, "Regional Peace Experience," 31.

30. Ibid.

31. Bouvier, *Civil Society Under Siege in Colombia*, 11.

32. Ibid.

The communities of Micoahumado and Tiquisio are both deeply involved in *Programa*-sponsored peace and economic development processes. We turn now to their more specific histories, which will include the crucial role that *Programa* has played.

MICOAHUMADO AND TIQUISIO

Micoahumado and Tiquisio are rural communities located in the southern part of the Bolivar *departamento* of Colombia. A *departamento* is similar to a state in the United States. The guerrilla group ELN traditionally claimed the Bolivar territory, but the FARC made inroads in recent years. As a result, there have been serious clashes with paramilitary groups, and Colombian security forces are especially active as well. Both Micoahumado and Tiquisio are on the front lines of the conflict, and both communities have years of experience with accompaniment by outside groups, both international and national. I conducted the case study of accompaniment, which is the centerpiece of this investigation, in these two communities.

Location of Bolivar Department of Colombia.

Micoahumado

Micoahumado is a regional center in the *municipio* of Morales, situated in the northeastern part of Colombia, not far from the Caribbean. The people cultivate coffee and various other kinds of beans, and mine for gold. The population of about seven thousand is *campesino*, living at a subsistence level without many basic services such as health care, secondary educa tion, and reliable electricity or phone service. The people there say that they feel abandoned by the state. They say the government invests in the war by sending its troops, but does not invest in community development.

Guerrillas showed up in the area in the 1970s and began dominating the region in the 1980s. People who had been living there for a long time, but still lacked proper titles to their land, feared the state would seize their farms from them, and so in the beginning many saw the guerrillas as a force that could protect them. And in the beginning, the guerrillas took on a social role, such as building schools and roads, in the absence of the state. However, as time passed, guerrilla groups became more powerful, more dominating, and more vertical in their organizational structure. People lost confidence in them, but there was no functioning state struc ture to replace them.

Beginning in the mid- to late 1990s paramilitary forces began incur sions into the area. Community leaders in Micoahumado report that the paramilitary forces are effectively illegally acting on behalf of the Colom bian armed forces. As noted earlier, paramilitary forces are responsible for most of the human rights violations attributed to the war.

One of the leaders in Micoahumado described to me his personal experiences with paramilitary forces. This man is an independent, small-scale artisan gold miner, and in the 1990s he had set up his own mining operation with two partners. Four times paramilitary forces entered the community where he was living with his wife and children, and four times the whole family had to flee, leaving behind everything. With the first displacement, he lost the small mining business he had spent ten years building. On the second occasion, paramilitary commanders captured him and took him, along with another community leader, to a slaughter house located on a riverbank. He was forced to watch while paramilitary forces used a chainsaw to cut his companion into pieces. The companion was alive when the chainsaw attack began, but mercifully he had a heart attack and lost consciousness. The miner managed to escape by jumping into the river. His capturers shot at him, but he survived, emerging down river hours later, bloody but alive. He and his family eventually ended up in Micoahumado, where he has become a leader in the community's fight for survival.

In December of 2002, six hundred paramilitary troops entered La Plaza, the central town in Micoahumado, occupied it, started burning it, and occupied the houses of civilians. In response, guerrilla forces, who were located in the surrounding forests, set up a blockade so that no food or medicine could enter, destroyed the town's water supply, and dropped bombs, several of which landed near the local elementary school.

Main street in La Plaza, Micoahumado's town center.

The townspeople had survived a number of such operations, and many people, like the man described above, had survived multiple displacements. But the 2002 occupation was worse than most, and community leaders agreed that something had to be done. Some people wanted to flee, but many had nowhere else to go, and some were tired of running. There has been so much displacement in Colombia that the entire *campesino* way of life is at risk. But this community was determined to preserve their lifestyle, and on their terms.

Town leaders called in the parish priest, Padre Joachim. Padre Joachim had spent the previous several years helping the community to organize what they call a Constituent Assembly, although it was this very serious paramilitary confrontation that served as the catalyst to finally formalize it. The Assembly is essentially a representative body that works together to solve local problems. The first step in organizing the Assembly was to survey the people, to determine their dreams and their thoughts about the future. The Assembly was born of the desires of the people, and organized to fulfill them. Because of the assembly, the people of Micoahumado had some experience working to jointly solve problems, and they had a leadership structure in place.

The leadership also called in Padre Francisco, the Jesuit director of *Programa de Desarrollo y Paz de Magdalena Medio*. *Programa* had been working in the community since 1995 to help residents come up with their own economic development plans, independently of any armed groups. It was *Programa* that later invited international accompaniment, including Christian Peacemaker Teams, to Micoahumado.

Padre Joachim and Padre Pacho (the peoples' name for Francisco DeRoux) sat down with community leaders and together they devised a plan for dialogue with the armed groups. The community formed a "com mission on dialogue," and, along with accompaniment by the Catholic Church and other national and international groups, held conversations with all of the armed groups, including the Colombian armed forces. They began with the guerrilla forces, and got them to agree to fix the water sup ply and leave the area. The paramilitaries agreed to leave if the guerrilla would leave. As a result, the community has not seen any serious violence since. All the armed groups are still present in the area, but they are not ac tively threatening Micoahumado. The next chapter discusses this further.

Today the community continues to work on its own economic devel opment plans, but still without the presence of the state.

Tiquisio

Tiquisio is a *municipio* located in the same general area as Michoahumado: in the southern Bolivar *departamento* in the region near the Magdalena Medio River. To reach Tiquisio, one has to travel by jeep over poorly main tained mountain roads, or go by boat. Twenty thousand people inhabit Tiquisio. Twenty-four percent of the population is of African descent. The impoverished and mostly rural population survives on small-scale agriculture, livestock, fishing, and small-scale, independent gold mining. In their own words, "What is certain is that abandonment by the state, the worsening of the armed conflict (displacement, kidnappings, selective executions, the stigmatization of the population, and extortion on the part of armed groups), along with poor communication with other *municipios*, have contributed to economic deterioration and, of course, to the destruction of the social fabric."[33]

This community's story is similar to that of Micoahumado. The region has suffered for most of its existence due to the absence of state structures. During the 1980s, that void was filled by the guerrilla movement. People had no choice but to ally themselves with the guerrillas because they were the only authority in existence. As a result, during the 1990s, with the arrival of paramilitary groups, community leaders were "stigmatized" by the government and accused of collaborating with the guerrillas. Authority then fluctuated between the guerrillas and the paramilitary forces, with the sporadic appearance of the Colombian army. In the late 1990s there was frequent open combat, and there were numerous civilian casualties.[34]

During the first half of June 2003, three civilians were assassinated by guerrilla forces, and as a result the community nearly displaced completely. After the assassinations, the Colombian army came into Coco Tiquisio, one of the *corregimientos*, or larger towns, of Tiquisio, and occupied the Catholic parish and school buildings. The parish center in Coco Tiquisio serves the entire *municipio* of Tiquisio. The military occupation led to a confrontation between the Diocese of Magangue and the Colombian military, because the diocese asserted that it is a violation of international law to station troops in civilian population areas. The army eventually evacuated the site, but some members of the military clandestinely began a campaign to discredit the Catholic parish, and this amplified the fear in the population.[35] Today the army is stationed on a hilltop overlooking the town center, still too close to the population center to be in compliance with international norms.

As a result of these events in June 2003, the Diocese of Magangue initiated a "Mission of Peace" in Coco Tiquisio, and, guided by their pastor, Padre Rafael Gallego, this peace mission led to a proposal for permanent accompaniment in Tiquisio, and for the initiation of the Tiquisio Citizens' Process (*Proceso Ciudadano Por Tiquisio*). As was the case with Micoahumado, *Programa de Desarrollo y Paz de Magdalena Medio* provided permanent accompaniment, and *Programa* later invited international accompaniment by CPT.

---

33. Parroquia del Santísimo Cristo de Tiquisio y Programa de Desarrollo y Paz de Magdalena Medio, *Proceso Ciudadano Por Tiquisio*, 19.

34. Ibid., 28–29.

35. Ibid., 30.

Main Street, Coco Tiquisio after December 2008 floods.

The Tiquisio Citizen's Process had beginnings similar to those of Mi choahumado's Constituent Assembly: *Programa* asked people about their hopes and dreams. After surveying the community, the leadership named three specific goals:

- Respect for and defense of life;

- The construction of community, including the right to remain on their territories;

- Work for overcoming the stigmatization of the community.

With the foundation of the Citizens' Process, Tiquisio declared itself a community in civil resistance. The main idea was to organize and unite themselves as a community, in order to resist the influence of armed groups and to devote themselves to the social, economic, and educational work that the state had failed to provide, because it was this void that armed groups had arrived to fill. The community realized that in order to survive, it had to fill the void itself.[36] The animator and manager of this process was, and still is, the *Santisimo Cristo* parish, led by their pastor, Padre Rafael Gallego.

36. Ibid., 32, 28.

Santisimo Cristo Church, Coco Tiquisio

Padre Raphael Gallego

Padre Rafael has played a crucial and innovative role in the Tiquisio process. One aspect of his leadership important to highlight is the way in which he has kept alive the memory of the community's missing and fallen, as a way to both remember and overcome the trauma. Each year in June Tiquisio's Catholic parish holds an annual community day that begins with a liturgy honoring the dead and disappeared. Their names are read aloud, and parishioners hold banners listing the names. In addition, the long list of dead and disappeared from the community is maintained permanently on banners hung on either side of the cross on the altar of the church. The community day in June is a time for the the people of Tiquisio not only to remember but also to remind themselves, through ritual and celebration, that they have moved forward. They have not perished as a community; rather, they have been reborn through the Citizens' Process.

The names of the three fallen civilians from June 2003, along with a statue of Mary, on the altar of Parroquia Santisimo Cristo in Tiquisio.

Like Micoahumado, today Tiquisio has a well-thought-out economic development and social service plan. Unfortunately, the state is still not present to help citizens execute it. They also continue to be accompanied by *Programa* and by Christian Peacemaker Teams. There have been no major paramilitary incursions since 2000, and no major guerrilla incursions since June 2003, although both groups maintain a presence outside the populated areas, especially in places where coca is grown.[37] The Colombian Armed Forces have maintained a constant presence in Coco Tiquisio since June 2003.

CONCLUSION

This chapter has endeavored to provide an overview of the cultural and historical factors—national, regional, and local—that relate to the interviews and case study in chapter 2. We have seen that the conflict in Colombia is complicated, with multiple national and international actors in play. The conflict has created a humanitarian disaster, with some estimates placing the number of displaced at 5.4 million. Civilian casualties continue, along with threats, abuses, and intimidation of rural populations and ethnic groups long marginalized by the Colombian state. There is widespread agreement in civil society that this conflict will not be resolved through military means, but rather by eradicating the economic disparities that scar the country.

Chapter 2 illustrates how two tiny communities have taken matters into their own hands by developing transparent and democratic leadership and economic development programs. It also shows how they have coped with open violence, threats, intimidation, and economic deprivation, how they have reconstituted themselves as communities, and the role that international accompaniment has played in their successes.

37. Ibid., 20.

2

Sustaining Life

First, and above all, we are defending our way of life, not with arms, but with ideas . . .

—DELIA CASTRO, TIQUISIO

INTRODUCTION

THIS CHAPTER EXAMINES THE ways that two communities in Colombia—Micoahumado and Tiquisio—have overcome violence, intimidation, and pressure to displace, and recreated themselves as thriving and self-governing communities. It will focus especially on the role of international accompaniment, and in particular accompaniment by Christian Peacemaker Teams (CPT), in supporting these communities in accomplishing their goals. Looking at international accompaniment will also shed light on other community processes that have led to their successes.

I interviewed a total of twenty-one leaders: twelve from Micoahumado, seven from Tiquisio, and two from *Programa de Desarrollo y Paz de Magdalena Medio*. A complete list of the names and functions of the interviewees can be found in the bibliography. I asked them why they invited international accompaniment to their communities. Specifically, I asked them to tell me about what the international accompaniers their communities, what are accompaniment's *effects* in their communities, and what is the *role* of international accompaniment. Role means what distinguishes international accompaniment from accompaniment by local, regional, or national groups. I also asked them to talk about the specifically Christian nature of CPT and whether that makes a difference to them and/or to the nature of the accompaniment. Finally, I asked them for suggestions to improve the quality of international accompaniment. All interviews were conducted in Spanish, and all translations are my own. I have both tapes and transcripts of the interviews.

I was able to get only seven interviews in Tiquisio because, during the time of my visit, one of the central Tiquisio towns, Coco Tiquisio, was suffering from extreme flooding. Further, one interviewee in Micoahumado declined to be taped, and two others became so nervous on tape that it was difficult to use their comments. However, there was nearly complete agreement among all the interviewees, including those who did not record well or who declined to be recorded, on the answers to my questioning. The ways that people told the stories may have varied slightly, but the interviewees, who represented the major leadership groups in both communities, were in nearly total agreement about the value of international accompaniment.

In the process of answering my questions, interviewees provided an enormous amount of information about the history of their communities and the impact of the conflict on themselves and their neighbors. For that reason, by the end of this chapter, the reader will have a very good picture of what a community-led peace process looks like, and how an international Christian group can support it.

WHY INVITE INTERNATIONAL ACCOMPANIMENT?

Accompaniers are those who are in every moment standing with us. Whatever happens, they stand with us.

—Pablo Santiago, Micoahumado

I asked this question to members of the community leadership in Tiquisio, including an extensive interview with Padre Rafael Gallego, and Micoahumado, as well as to Padre Francisco DeRoux, SJ, and to Ubencel Duque, his associate director at *Programa*. In 2003 Padre Joachim of Micoahumado received very serious death threats from paramilitary forces and his bishop removed him from Colombia altogether, and for that reason I could not interview him. Another part of the question is: why specifically Christian accompaniment? There are other accompaniment groups; most of the others are human rights groups with no religious affiliation. Does Christian accompaniment bring something that the other groups do not bring?

I received five main categories of answers:

1. Outside accompaniment makes the community feel less isolated and less alone in their struggle. This feeling gives them the strength to continue working for their own survival, rather than displacing, be cause it validates the community's own projects to sustain life. Ac companiers affirm the dignity and value of the community and its members. This feeling is a result of ongoing presence and relation ship with the accompanying groups, and was the answer to the ques tion: what do the accompaniers *do*. What they do is to be present in relationship.

2. Outside accompaniment provides a kind of "umbrella" that covers local people, who believe that killing someone from outside the re gion would exact a political cost that the armed groups, especially those affiliated with the Colombian state, would not want to pay. For this reason, it diminishes the activity of armed groups. This was one of the answers to the question: what are the *effects* of international accompaniment.

3. Outside accompaniment opens up space in the communities for so cial and political organizing, dialogue with armed actors, preserva tion of the communities by preventing displacement, and economic development. This was a second set of answers to the questioning about *effects*.

4. Outside accompaniment provides witnesses. These witnesses can tell the community's story to the international community, to other NGOs and churches, to the press, and to foreign governments, es pecially the United States, whose policies profoundly affect how the conflict is conducted. Everyone I spoke to assumed that this is part of the work of Christian Peacemaker Teams. The people see this as addressing one of the root causes of the violence. This was the chief answer to the question about the *role* of international accompani ment, as opposed to the role of accompaniment by local, regional, or national organizations.

5. Outside accompaniment, especially Christian accompaniment, edu cates the community. CPT brings in Christian values, such as non violence and respect for human life, that are immensely important

in a conflict zone. In a context where dialogue is needed, Christian values demand that all people are respected equally. In a context where young people are joining armed groups out of either poverty or revenge, Christian values teach that there is an option to choose nonviolence. Christian values also teach them that they have human rights, and they have a right to demand that those rights be respected. This was in response to the question of the value of specifically *Christian* accompaniment.

The following sections treat each of these answers in some depth, and addresses the suggestions of these leaders for improving international accompaniment.

ACCOMPANIMENT AS PRESENCE

It seems to me that the greatest and most positive impact of accompaniment is that the communities perceive themselves as accompanied, and so feel that they are not alone.

—JORGE TAFUR, TIQUISIO

Without exception, every person I interviewed talked about how critical it is that these isolated and marginalized communities feel they are not alone in their struggle for survival. Most people named this as the single most important aspect of accompaniment, whether it comes from national or international groups. "Please don't leave us alone" was a plea repeated often, and by most interviewees.

Although presence is cited as what the international accompaniers *do*, presence itself has profound *effects* on the psyche of the community. The presence of outside accompaniment makes the communities feel secure and protected, and this gives them the courage to persist in their own projects to sustain life in their own villages. It gives the people confidence that their project for survival is a valid one, and that their way of life is worth preserving.

> When (the accompanier) arrives and converses with one of us, they give courage; one feels in the body how to endure, how to survive . . . it gives us hope.[1]

---

1. Doña Maria (last name withheld), interview with author, December 12, 2008.

This sense of security makes people more willing to "move forward," in stead of giving up, displacing, or even becoming part of the conflict. context of massive internal displacement, this impact of accompaniment, according to Ubencel Duque of *Programa*, "contributes to affirming the decision of the community to continue living in their territory, not just in any kind of a way, but rather with dignity."[3]

ACCOMPANIMENT PROVIDES AN "UMBRELLA" THAT DIMINISHES VIOLENCE

The ELN and the paramilitaries and the armed forces knew that to kill a foreigner from the United States or Canada or Europe, who was providing service to the community . . . well, it was very difficult to touch such a person from the outside. In some way this constitutes a kind of deterrent, a kind of umbrella.

—FRANCISCO DEROUX, SJ

Nearly everyone I interviewed believes that the presence of international accompaniment has been a factor in decreasing the activities of armed actors in their communities. Most concede that the violence has not com pletely disappeared, but they stress that it has diminished significantly.

> We are about to complete five years (of accompaniment) in June, and for four years a violent death has not been heard of in these zones. There have been a few isolated cases in the mu-nicipal center, but here, the part that was the most shaken up, it has diminished totally. So we consider that international ac-companiment has been an effective remedy.[4]

Some are not able to articulate exactly why, but many people, espe cially those leaders and clergy with a lot of organizing experience outside of the communities, believe that the presence of international groups acts as a deterrent to the armed groups: guerrilla, paramilitary, and Colombian armed forces alike. International accompaniment provides a deterrent be cause to violate or kill a member of an international group would lead to a high political cost for the armed groups: "We have found that international

2. Delia Castro, interview with author, December 7, 2008.
3. Ubencel Duque, interview with author, December 11, 2008.
4. Felix Villegas, interview with author, December 5, 2008.

accompaniment elevates the political cost for the actors who can intervene or who are intervening against the community."[5]

In Tiquisio and Micoahumado, leaders believe that this elevated political cost has caused some of the armed groups to withdraw completely, and others to be more careful in the ways they interact with the communities. In the case of Micoahumado, leaders believe that accompaniment led to the removal of the paramilitary forces altogether, and to the guerrillas ceding "a lot of space" to the community. By ceding space, they mean that guerrillas still enter the town to shop and to drink, but they are no longer giving the orders, and they no longer act in a disorderly manner.[6]

Tiquisio leaders perceive similar results with the guerrilla and paramilitary forces. "If you all had not been present, I think that the armed groups, legal as well as illegal, would always be trying to intimidate the people."[7] They also believe that the behavior of the Colombian armed forces has improved as a result of accompaniment. Speaking about the activities of the Colombian military, Padre Rafael Gallego stated:

> We feel that the war efforts have been stopped or have not affected the civilian population as severely as before . . . For that reason we place great value on international accompaniment.[8]

This is significant, because it is not necessarily the presence of the armed forces that presents a problem, but rather their treatment of the civilian population. Leaders explained that as a result of guerrilla activity in the area, the Colombian armed forces would catalogue the entire community as members of the guerrilla forces and treat them as criminals, violating their human rights.[9]

In general people seem to feel that all the armed groups are more respectful of human rights with the presence of international accompaniment.

> Accompaniment has . . . helped us to achieve our goals, because they are working on behalf of human rights, and this makes the armed groups respect human rights. Groups carrying arms have had to resort to respecting human rights.[10]

5. Padre Rafael Gallego, interview with author, December 4, 2008.

6. Julio Arbolera and Pablo Santiago, interviews with author, December 12, 2008.

7. Felix Villegas, interview with author.

8. Padre Rafael Gallego, interview with author.

9. Personal interview with Felix Villegas.

10. Personal interview with Julio Arbolera.

Several leaders suggested that Christian groups provide a particularly important witness for respecting human rights, and that it is the fact the CPT is Christian that has shamed the armed groups into behaving better. Speaking about the activities of the military, which is responsible, whether directly or indirectly, for the bulk of the human rights violations in Colombia, Ubencal Duque of *Programa* remarked:

> When they realize that who stands before them are men and women of faith, of commitment, and who are not just committed locally, but who have a universal commitment, and who are men and women in a missionary role, this makes them realize that there are men and women here in Colombia suffering under degrading situations. I think that the public institutions have had to recognize this and have had to redefine the way they act. I think that this says a lot about the role of CPT in this region.[11]

Put another way, community leaders perceive that in places where there is no international accompaniment, there are more human rights violations.[12] Community leaders believe that international accompaniment has the effect of diminishing the activities of armed groups in their communities, leading to a reduction in violence and human rights abuse.

INTERNATIONAL ACCOMPANIMENT MAKES SPACE FOR COMMUNITY PROCESSES

What accompaniment does is simply contribute to creating the space, to creating the conditions, so that God manifests, through the Spirit, in some men and women who are suppressed and living under difficult restrictions. A good accompanier contributes to lifting the restrictions so that this manifestation of God can be seen.

—Francisco DeRoux, SJ

Diminishing or decreasing the activities of armed groups opens up the possibility for communities to think about something other than pure survival. In the case of Micoahumado and Tiquisio, it has enabled them to construct community-organizing processes with a democratic leadership structure. This, in turn, has enabled them to begin to reweave their

11. Personal interview with Ubencel Duque.
12. Personal interview with Delia Castro.

destroyed social fabric, to gain concessions through dialogue with armed groups, and to begin to develop their own economic development plans. Although led by the communities themselves, all of this progress was supported and sustained through ongoing accompaniment by local, regional, and international groups.

Community Organizing

Chapter 1 briefly described the Tiquisio Citizens' Process and the Micoahumado Constituent Assembly. The arrival of accompaniment, the diminishment of the activities of armed groups, and organizing the two community processes happened together, and most people I spoke with saw them as one and the same process. In both cases, it happened in 2003.

In Tiquisio, Padre Rafael Gallego was appointed to be pastor of Parroquilla Santisimo Cristo, located in the village of Coco Tiquisio, that year. Padre Rafael describes how the people developed their own goals for the process:

> So, the (accompaniment) institutions asked the people of Tiquisio what they wanted, what they were feeling, what worried them. The people said: "First, life. We need that the right to life is guaranteed, and the right to continue living on our lands. We also need, along with life, the right to our land, and food security: we need food." . . . There was a two-fold path: we are going to preserve life, while demanding that we stay on our lands and reconstruct our ruined community.[13]

All of the people I interviewed in Tiquisio confirmed that this was a process that surged from the community itself, and, with strong support from outside accompaniment, has empowered the community. The end result of this process was that the community was able to change its story from one of violence, stigmatization, displacement, and a destroyed social fabric, to one of hope, community organizing, and economic development.

> First and foremost (the process) changed our history. Our social organizations had been stigmatized by the state. But we wanted to show them that in our *municipios* there is not only war; there are also ways to make peace, to construct peace . . . From 1998 until the present, through stigmatization, the state and also the paramilitaries were breaking all of the social order that we had in our communities. They changed beginning in 2003, as a result

13. Personal interview with Padre Rafael Gallego.

of Programa de Desarrollo y Paz de Magdalena Medio and of Padre Rafael Gallego, and of many other persons who believe in the proposal of the communities to reclaim our social fabric.[14]

The community believes that it remains alive today as a result of the Citizens' Process, and Tiquisio's leaders cannot conceive of the Citizens' Process without the presence of outside accompaniment. Outside accompaniment not only helped them to learn how to organize themselves; it also helped them to believe in themselves. That outside accompaniment takes the form of local accompaniment (the Catholic Church), regional accompaniment (*Programa* and others), and international accompaniment (CPT).

The story of the Micoahumado Constituent Assembly is similar, except that the local pastor who initiated it was not Padre Rafael, but rather Padre Joachim Mayorga. *Programa* had been working with the campesinos in Micoahumado since 1996, encouraging them to develop as a community independently of the guerrilla and paramilitary forces. According to Padre Francisco DeRouz, SJ, then director of *Programa*, the work was very difficult. Community leaders were not sure they could trust *Programa* and many had placed their confidence in the guerrillas, because there was no other functioning authority. But slowly, over time, *Programa* was able to create an environment in the community where everyone understood that there was an alternative to violence to solve their problems. *Programa* was able to convince them to work together to overcome injustice, poverty, and violence.[15]

In this context, Padre Joachim arrived in Micoahumado, and the Constituent Assembly was born. Padre Joachim, working from a base of liberation theology, began to organize "Missions of Peace" in Micoahumado. Missions of Peace were seminars and educational programs confirming the community's commitment to peace. Padre Francisco DeRoux tells the story of how the Constituent Assembly came to be:

> In December 2002, Padre Joachim was in Micoahumado conducting a Mission of Peace with the people when the paramilitary forces entered the area. When the paramilitaries arrived, they entered into the building where the Mission was taking place. Padre Joachim continued with the Mission, but Padre Joachim and the other leaders called me to accompany them. The situation was complicated. The paramilitaries were in the

14. Personal interview with Delia Castro.

15. Padre Francisco DeRoux, SJ, interview with author, December 18, 2008

middle of the village, and every day a helicopter arrived with food for the paramilitaries. The guerrilla was outside of the village, and the guerrilla destroyed the aqueduct, and they fired two bombs that landed next to the school. In this context we saw that we had to talk to both groups.

In that moment Padre Joachim began to construct the Constituent Assembly of Micoahumado. The Assembly increased the political participation of the people. It was an initiative of Padre Joachim . . . Through the Assembly, the people learned to dialogue over internal matters. Through the Assembly, an atmosphere was created that the people realized they had to do something, and a commission of dialogue was formed.[16]

Similar to Tiquisio, the people of Micoahumado believe that the Constituent Assembly has enabled them to survive.

Those of us who have remained here, have remained because we organized ourselves into social organizations supporting life and not war, meaning that we support life, we love life, and we fight for life. In 2003, we initiated a path of defense of life on our lands, and on that path we remain.[17]

Outside accompaniment, including international accompaniment, invited by Padre Joachim and Padre Pacho, was essential to the work of the Constituent Assembly from the beginning. Because the accompaniment organizations were present from the beginning, it is impossible for people from Micoahumado to separate the work of accompaniment from the work of the Constituent Assembly. They are part of the same process. In this way, international accompaniment has strengthened the local community organizations.

International accompaniment not only has strengthened local social organizations, but has also helped to make possible the work of regional groups such as *Programa de Desarrollo y Paz de Magdalena Medio*, which, as we have seen, has been crucial to the rebirth of these communities. According to Ubencel Duque, Associate Director of *Programa*, "when we feel accompanied, including feeling accompanied ourselves, it makes us more daring." [18] In other words, in a context where human rights workers are at extreme risk, it gives them the courage to continue their struggle on behalf of the rights of Colombia's marginalized communities.

16. Ibid.

17. Eugenio Gomez, interview with author, December 14, 2008.

18. Ubencel Duque, interview with author.

International accompaniment has helped to give birth to these democratic systems of self-governance in places where the government itself has historically not been present. This, in turn, has enabled the community-led economic development projects which have empowered these communities to stay on their territories.

Dialogue

As we have already seen, Micoahumado's community process, backed up by regional and international accompaniment, opened up the possibility of dialogue with armed groups: "The presence of those (accompaniment) groups made possible the dialogues. Without those groups of *gringos* dialogues would not have taken place."[19]

The first dialogues began on December 20, 2002, while the paramilitary forces were still occupying La Plaza, the central town in Micoahumado, and the guerrillas were outside the town, firing bombs. The guerrilla forces had a history of taking civilian hostages, and they had mined the roads and the town aqueduct, and imposed a blockade on the entry of food and medicine into the village. The first round of dialogues ended on the January 8, 2003. Julio Arbolera describes the content of the first dialogues:

> We told the guerrilla that what we were saying to them was the same thing we were saying to the others (the paramilitary forces), that they respect our human rights, and that we were civilians. We reminded them that we did not have anything to do with their confrontations, and we asked them to please allow us to have a peaceful Christmas and New Year. They accepted this. And then we met with the paramilitary forces and explained the same problems, because at that time they were sleeping in the houses of civilians, cooking and bathing in the houses of civilians. The first thing we told them was to vacate the village and not to harm civilians.[20]

Seventeen civilian members of the community participated as members of the original Commission on Dialogue, and they were accompanied by Padre Joachim, Padre Pacho and Ubencel Duque of *Programa*, a number of Colombian organizations, and CPT, which was present for many meetings but not all of them. Julio Arbolera was the community member

19. Ana Garay, interview with author, December 14, 2008.
20. Julio Arbolera, interview with author.

who initially organized the Commission on Dialogue. After the initial dialogues, both sides fulfilled their promises to vacate the village until after the New Year. In January, there were new confrontations between guerrilla and paramilitary forces, but very quickly afterward, the paramilitary forces left the region altogether.[21]

For the next two years, the Commission, along with its accompaniers, met regularly with guerrilla and paramilitary leadership. Padre Francisco De Roux reports that the group traveled to the *municipio* center, Morales, to talk with the mayor and with Colombian military officers, to inform them about the dialogues, and also to request their accompaniment. Both the mayor's office and the military officers were happy to hear about the dialogues, but they refused to participate. Padre Francisco remarked: "None of them dared to accompany the community. So it was the civilian population protecting the governmental institutions, without accompaniment from those institutions."[22]

The community won many concessions from both sides, including the permanent removal of paramilitary forces, the removal of the guerrillas to beyond the *municipio* boundaries, and the lifting of the blockades and restoration of the water supply. Although it took some time, the community was also able to get the guerrillas to remove the landmines. This was significant, because the landmines were placed in the roads, and made it impossible for inhabitants of smaller villages to move around the region or to trade.

Pablo Santiago tells the story of how it happened:

> We insisted to the guerrilla organization: "We need to introduce (economic) projects into the region, we need the roads in order to move vehicles and cargo, and you need to allow these roads to be used for peace, and not for war." It was like that, and after two years, in 2005, on December 28, in the afternoon we received a communication from the commander of the ELN that said that as a result of the demands of the community of Micoahumado, they were going to allow a humanitarian demining.[23]

The Colombian armed forces had also been committing abuses in the community, but the Commission on Dialogue changed the dynamics between the community and the military.

---

21. Ibid.

22. Padre Francisco DeRoux, SJ, interview with author.

23. Pablo Santiago, interview with author.

> The Commission on Dialogue went to Bucaramanga and met with the general commander of the military forces. We presented all of our complaints. As a result, he replaced the battalion with a different class of army. They were more formal, and kinder, respecting the communities. That's how it was. As a result of pressure from the leaders and from the communities, and of the complaints, we were able to bring about a change.[24]

As with Tiquisio, the community of Micoahumado believes that an important reason for its success has been the presence of outside ac companiment, from both national organizations and from CPT, and that in particular CPT's accompaniment led the government armed forces to respect civilian space. Padre Pacho suggests that, in addition to the ben efits of its presence, CPT played another important role in the dialogues. Because of CPT's spirituality, CPT has taught community members cer tain elements that were important in achieving success with the dialogue process. In particular, CPT taught them to respect all sides, and to listen to and understand their story, even if one personally is not in agreement with it.[25] We will return to the role of CPT's spirituality later in this chapter.

Tiquisio has not had the same experience of dialoguing with all the different armed groups, primarily because the Colombian armed forces have maintained a permanent base in the center of Coco Tiquisio since 2003, and this has kept out the other armed groups. However, Tiquisio's leaders do have some experience talking with the armed forces. Most re cently, Padre Rafael Gallego was the victim of threats from the paramili tary forces, and had to leave the region temporarily.

> In April of 2008, the paramilitaries generated a threat via the internet. A Commandante Camilo signed. There were two emails, supposedly signed by Commandante Camilo of the *Bloque Norte de Autodefenses*, a paramilitary force, in which we were called "workers of war." In the second communication, we were linked directly to the FARC.[26]

Out of fear, two lay pastoral workers departed permanently. However, Padre Rafael was able to return to Tiquisio and continue working after only a few months. He was able to return because, together with *grama*, he met with the Colombian armed forces and representatives of the Colombian government. As noted earlier, most people understand

24. Julio Arbolera, interview with author.
25. Padre Francisco DeRoux, SJ, interview with author.
26. Padre Rafael Gallego, interview with author.

that the paramilitary forces are illegally acting on behalf of the Colombian military. For that reason, Padre Rafael chose to interact with the military, rather than searching for "Commandante Camilo." Padre Rafael believes he was threatened because of his efforts to have the military base removed from the center of Coco Tiquisio.

> We explained to them our situation, the conditions in which we worked. *Programa* one more time explained all of its work in the zone, and the Vice President of the Republic said that he had not understood it, and that it had been necessary to understand it. And the military chiefs, especially in Barrancabermeja, said "it is important to understand this work," and we felt encouraged to continue working.[27]

In our conversations, Padre Rafael did not credit this success directly to the presence of international accompaniment in the zone. However, given all that we have seen so far, it seems reasonable to conclude that the presence of international accompaniment contributed to creating the conditions whereby such a dialogue could take place and be successful. What we have seen is that international accompaniment plays an important part in creating the conditions that enable local and regional social organizations to do their work, even in the midst of violent conflict.

Economic Development

> *It is really important to look at how to create employment in the zone, how to strengthen the economy. We have a huge number of youth who grow up without a single prospect for employment or education. They grow up without a horizon. I think that joining the guerrilla, and joining the paramilitaries, and also joining the official army, is a way to resolve their lives.*

—Padre Rafael Gallego, Tiquisio

In both Tiquisio and Micoahumado, strong local organizations, along with dramatic decreases in the activities of armed groups, made it possible for the communities to remain on their territory, rather than displacing, and this in turn opened up the space for economic development projects. This is crucial, because in a context where poverty is endemic, people are

---

27. Padre Rafael Gallego, interview with author.

looking for a way to sustain themselves, and according to nearly everyone I interviewed, this accounts for why most people decide to join armed groups: "Many young people join paramilitary groups because they pay a monthly salary of 700,000 or 800,000 pesos."[28]

Tiquisio

Food security is one of the objectives of the Tiquisio Citizen's Process. To achieve it, the Citizen's Process has established the *Granja Integral Auto sostenible La Esperanza de Tiquisio* (The Comprehensive, Self-Sustainable Hope Farm of Tiquisio). Hope Farm is situated on land left idle by a group of Franciscan missionaries who worked in the area from 1976 to They fled because they received serious death threats and had to abandon their planned development of agricultural projects.[29] Hope Farm is a community project operated by ninety-seven local families, and managed by eight coordinators and a general administrator. It currently is developing eight agricultural projects: egg production, chickens, pigs, goat milk, fish, cattle, sugar cane, and cacao.[30]

Padre Rafael Gallego helps to feed the chicks at Hope Farm.

28. Delia Castro, interview with author.

29. Parroquia del Santísimo Cristo de Tiquisio y Programa de Desarrollo y Paz de Magdalena Medio, *Proceso Ciudadano por Tiquisio*, 19.

30. Ibid., 54.

The community's hope for the future rests on this and other projects, but they have very little in the way of resources. Padre Rafael and other leaders told me that this project provides an alternative economic model, one founded on the needs of community, as opposed to the models of economic development that involve "mega-projects" that community members feel are being imposed on them by outside economic powers.

> Their model is of an "excluding" society, and is an accumulative model that, instead of dignifying human beings, impoverishes many. We understand very clearly that economic development does not mean opening up huge buildings, or constructing beautiful avenues or highways. We understand development to be when human beings have the minimum they need in order to live in dignity. This is true development.[31]

The leadership of Tiquisio wants the community to be responsible for its own economic development, and to do it on its own terms. They say that instead of an outside corporation coming into the region and buying up land and resources, which they then exploit for their own profit, the community wants to develop its own resources, and to reap the benefits of its own work. Although outside corporations sometimes bring in jobs, usually those jobs are low-paying and do not raise people out of poverty.

Padre Rafael would like to see international accompaniment expand to include a kind of economic solidarity. The community has begun economic development only on a small scale, and Tiquisio needs financial resources to continue. But Padre Rafael's vision is one of accompaniment and long-term relationship, not just sending an annual check. He would like a church group or organization with resources to take a long-term interest in Tiquisio, to visit the people who live there, to pray with them, to work with them, to provide formation and training, and to help with the finances.[32]

Micoahumado

Micoahumado's dreams and goals are similar, although the community is a bit further along in achieving them. Micoahumado was one of the first projects of *Programa*, and through the work of *Programa* it received some outside investment from Japan. The Constituent Assembly, which

---

31. Jorge Tafur, interview with author, December 7, 2008.
32. Padre Rafael Gallego, interview with author.

has about one hundred sixty members, formed standing committees, and one of those committees focuses on economic production. Through its work, a cooperative, called ASOPROMIL (*Asociación Productiva de Mi coahumado*), was formed. The cooperative purchases the products of its members and sells them to buyers, searching for the best prices. The co operative started working only with sugar cane, cacao and cattle, but has expanded to include coffee, beans, and grains. Together its members have been able to find better and more reliable prices for the crops that were already being produced in the area.[33]

Pablo Santiago in the ASOPROMIC offices.

33. Pablo Santiago, Treasurer of ASOPROMIL, interview with author, December 14, 2008.

ASOPROMIC Storage building for beans and grains. Pictured are Juan Bautista Colorado, Eugenio Gomez, and an unknown member of the cooperative.

Wilson Ropero and Arisolina Rodriguez with bags of coffee.

The community also has big, but as of yet unfulfilled, dreams about coffee production. Micoahumado's leaders want their community to be come known as a coffee-producing region in Colombia, and they want to package and sell coffee under their own label. Unfortunately, their desire to roast and package it themselves has stalled, and they say they need more training. Like Tiquisio's leaders, they are looking for outside investment and relationship.[34]

Leaders in both communities, Tiquisio and Micoahumado, made a special effort to show me the community's economic development proj ects, and they talked about the projects as their community's hope for the future. These projects are symbols of the new life these communities have gained through their efforts at organizing and dialoguing, and all of these efforts have been sustained and supported through the presence of outside accompaniment. Economic development is part of the overall project to sustain the life and dignity of the community and its members.

ACCOMPANIMENT PROVIDES WITNESSES

Nearly everyone I spoke with emphasized that the crucial function, or role, of international accompaniment is witnessing and reporting. They believe that the reason why armed groups, legal as well as illegal, show so much "respect" in the presence of international accompaniment is that they know that international groups will report abuses, both within Co lombia and to the international community. In other words, international accompaniers witness the situation of the community through their pres ence, and then report violations and abuses to national and international authorities who have control over outcomes in Colombia, and it is this threat of reporting that lowers the risk of violence in the communities where international accompaniment is present. This is the value, or role, of "international eyes and ears."[35]

One form of witnessing and reporting involves filing complaints with regional and national governmental authorities tasked with ensuring that the Colombian government respects human rights. This is important because the majority of the human rights violations are committed by either paramilitary forces tied to the Colombian government, or by the Colombian armed forces. However, CPT does not necessarily file those

34. Wilson Ropero, Manager of the ASOPROMIL coffee project, interview with author, December 15, 2008.

35. Padre Rafael Gallego, interview with author.

complaints itself. Rather, CPT's accompaniment opens up the space for local and regional organizations to file the complaints, because it makes them more daring. As one leader put it, the presence of CPT makes it impossible for the Colombian state to tell lies about human rights violations, because CPT can witness to the truth.[36]

Community leaders name a specific role for CPT of reporting abuses and violations to the press, and to the embassies and government officials of their countries of origin. This, in turn, puts pressure on Colombian authorities, because Colombia is dependent on the financial assistance of other countries to sustain its internal war. In the words of Padre Francisco DeRoux, this reporting to the outside makes the authorities "uncomfortable."[37] It makes them uncomfortable because it threatens their financial base.

Community leaders told me that they expect CPT to publicize their situation internationally, and to pressure their governments to change policies in Colombia. It is the threat of doing so that makes the armed groups, especially the paramilitary and military forces, "respect" the presence of CPT.

CPT'S SPIRITUALITY VALUABLE
IN A CONFLICT ZONE

A few people talked about the spirituality of CPT as what sets it apart from other accompaniment groups. This was in response to questioning about the difference between accompaniment from a Christian group, and accompaniment from groups without a religious base. I found that it is not just CPT's Christianity that people view as important; rather, it is the quality of its Christianity. Those who answered this question were enthusiastic about these distinct but related spiritual aspects of CPT's accompaniment that are shared by very few other accompaniment groups: its ecumenical character, its spirituality of nonviolence, and its manner of connecting faith to acting on behalf of the human rights of others. The first two issues were mentioned as particularly important by CPT's main inviting organization, *Program de Desarrollo y Paz de Magdalena Medio*, and the last issue by four of the six women I interviewed. Others mentioned the need for more education and formation in leadership and economic development, but did not connect it to spirituality as such.

36. Jorge Tafur, interview with author.
37. Padre Francisco DeRoux, SJ, interview with author.

CPT's Ecumenical Identity

Padre Rafael Gallego spoke extensively about the importance of an ac companiment that is comprised of Christians of different denominations and confessions, because this strengthens and encourages the participa tion of non-Catholics in the community's work. He viewed it as important that the accompaniers live their faith together with the people, praying together and working together. He stressed the importance of the accom paniers making their faith visible to the community, so that it can be seen that they are working from a base of faith. He saw this as a kind of witness to how people of different Christian traditions can work together and live together peacefully, without competing with each other or insisting that others convert to their point of view. He stated that although non-Cath olics participate in the Tiquisio community processes and celebrations, they are less involved in them than the Catholics in the community, and the presence of CPT encourages them to participate.

Ubencel Duque and Francisco DeRoux, SJ, of *Programa*, echoed Pa dre Rafael's sentiments about the importance of an ecumenical witness in a zone of conflict. This is because armed groups are able to exploit divi sions, religious or otherwise, in order to divide the community and thus undermine its unifying community processes and thereby exert control.

Spirituality of Nonviolence

Padre Francisco DeRoux, SJ, spoke particularly eloquently about CPT's spirituality of nonviolence, emphasizing the importance of presenting an alternative to violence in a zone where young people join armed groups as a solution to poverty and hopelessness.

> CPT arrived and quickly demonstrated the quality of their spirituality. In *Programa* we felt very inspired by them. They did not have a political position, and they did not come in order to search for political influence, or prestige, or recognition, but rather sought to achieve reconciliation and peace. They brought a few very strong messages about the defense of human life, and seeking solutions through dialogue, and a very deep Christian spirituality. I felt personally called to talk with them, because *Programa* needed this type of spirituality. CPT brought

a theological and mystical dimension that led us to deepen our
own efforts . . . It was very radical, and very clear.[38]

Referring to CPT's "spiritual mission," Padre Francisco went on to
say that CPT demonstrates, in a way that is based in the Gospel, how to act
in the middle of violent conflict. This manner of acting respects the dignity of all, and listens to the perspective of all, even those with whom they
do not agree. This is a "radical" option on behalf of the human person.[39]

Taking an option for the human person in turn leads to the growth
of the community, continued Padre Francisco. CPT accompanies communities "in pain," who have been subjected to enormous suffering. The
fact that it offers itself, with humility and respect, to the communities,
contributes to their personal and spiritual growth. It causes them to give
the best of themselves, rather than giving up. Referring to the first time he
and I met, when I was accompanying a group of miners after one of their
leaders was assassinated by the Colombian military, Padre Francisco said:

> For example, when you were with those miners after the assas-
> sination of Alejandro Uribe, what were you doing? You were
> giving testimony that you believed in those men and women.
> And those men and women, because they felt accepted and rec-
> ognized, gave the best of themselves.[40]

According to him, this point is central, because it encourages people to
seek nonviolent solutions that are not based in revenge. This is a kind
of a spiritual presence that cannot be measured but that should not be
underestimated.

Ubencel Duque zeroed in on this issue as well. He stated that he views
CPT's work as essentially Christian evangelizing, but not in the sense that
it is commonly understood. CPT "goes to the root of the issues that cause
division and puts them into a perspective of unity. CPT demonstrates that
our actions should not generate dispute and division, because these are
what lead to violence. CPT is evangelizing communities mired in years of
conflict, with Christian values that promote nonviolence."[41] Padre Rafael
Gallego also told me that he believes this type of spirituality is a kind of

---

38. Padre Francisco DeRoux, SJ, interview with author.

39. Ibid.

40. Ibid.

41. Ubencel Duque, interview with author.

positive Christian evangelization that supports and lifts up the work of the local church.[42]

Formation

Four of the six women I interviewed talked about the importance of the formation they received from their accompaniers. However, I am address ing it under the topic of spirituality because they are not talking about for mation in some kind of technical skill. Rather, they are referring to what Padre Francisco talks about above: the accompaniers have taught these women that they have dignity as human beings, and as such, have rights and the responsibility to fight for them. Arisolina Rodriquez of Michoa humado said it powerfully:

> For me, accompaniment, both national and international, has been so important because I have learned so much from them. I have learned to defend any kind of humanitarian concern that comes up in the community. I am ready for it because thanks to the accompaniers I now have the capacity . . . I defend the rights of any citizen because I now know what our rights are.[43]

Doña Maria, the matriarch of Micoahumado, expressed it as a kind of "waking up" of the community. The community had been asleep, and the accompaniers arrived, and "threw cold water on us . . . They gave us a light, and a voice, and the power to survive more than what we had thought we could."[44]

This waking up of the communities included workshops on human rights, most of which were conducted by Colombian organizations, such as *Programa*. However, as I noted earlier, the work of *Programa* is enabled and reinforced by the presence of CPT and other international groups.

SUGGESTIONS

I asked people if they had any suggestions for improving the quality of international accompaniment, and of CPT's presence in particular. Al though all were extraordinarily grateful for CPT's work, they were not shy about offering suggestions for improvement. Their suggestions fall into

42. Padre Rafael Gallego, interview with author.

43. Arisolina Rodriquez, interview with author, December 16, 2008.

44. Doña Maria (last name withheld), interview with author.

two categories of requests: a more permanent presence in the communities, and more effort toward supporting future economic development.

A More Permanent Presence

Nearly all the community leaders in Tiquisio and Micoahumado wanted CPT to maintain a permanent presence, either in their communities or in their region, the southern part of the Department of Bolivar. CPT's permanent office is located in the city of Barrancabermeja, and it takes a full day or more of travel by boat and then by jeep to arrive at either of the two communities. CPT's urban location enables its volunteers to spread out more widely and accompany more communities.

However, as Delia Castro and others pointed out, the main role of CPT is to witness to abuses and rights violations, and to report them to national and international authorities, and one cannot report on violations that one does not see, and one cannot see them if one is not present.[45] Padre Rafael added that serious human rights violations happen between the visits of CPT, and for that reason it would be better for the communities if CPT maintained a permanent presence, as a deterrent.[46] Pablo Santiago stated his feeling that an added benefit of a full-time presence in the community is that CPT could strengthen the community's effort to keep young people from collaborating with any of the armed groups.[47]

Everyone I spoke with recognized that the reason CPT makes only sporadic visits is because they do not have the personnel for a full-time presence. They are spreading themselves thin, in the hopes of doing the most good for the most people. While understanding that, the people express a strong hope that at some point CPT will find a way to live permanently with the communities. This would involve a dramatic increase in personnel and in funding for the work of groups like CPT.

Training and Economic Development

A number of the men I interviewed thought that international accompaniment should strengthen their efforts at economic development. The reason for this is because community-led economic development projects

45. Delia Castro, interview with author.
46. Padre Rafael Gallego, interview with author.
47. Pablo Santiago, interview with author.

are their hope for pulling themselves out of poverty, and they believe it is poverty that is driving people, especially young men, to join armed groups, and therefore poverty is driving the conflict.

They suggest that a starting point for this would be finding ways to provide technical assistance, or training. For example, Wilson Ropero, who is in charge of Micoahumado's coffee project, told me that they lost an opportunity to further develop their coffee project last year because they did not know enough about the business.

> The fundamental thing is that we need more training . . . Last year we had a (coffee) project, almost approved, but we did not have enough experience in the industry. We started the project but we did not have any knowledge of how to develop it . . . I am asking you to come here with technical assistance, because we have failed without it.[48]

Others echoed Wilson's sentiments about the need for training in order to move forward. Using the example of floods that had recently dev astated Tiquisio, Padre Rafael illustrated the point:

> For example, right now, with the floods, people from the outside are bringing in food and clothing. The floods will pass, but the people here remain in the same situation. And next year there will be another flood, and the national and international solidarity will return, and we repeat the same thing. We think that accompaniment, both national and international, should go to the root of the problem, which is the economic inequality that this country suffers under.[49]

In other words, international accompaniment is excellent as far as it goes, but CPT's current way of practicing it does not get to the root of the conflict, which is economic inequality, and as long as the economic inequality continues, the conflict continues in one form or another.

CONCLUSION:
THE IMPORTANCE OF COLLABORATION

The communities of Micoahumado and Tiquisio, as well as the regional organization *Programa de Desarrollo y Paz de Magdelana Medio*, the work of Christian Peacemaker Teams very, very highly. The presence

48. Wilson Ropero, interview with author.
49. Padre Rafael Gallego, interview with author.

of international accompaniment affects the psyche of the communities, as well as that of Colombian human rights workers, making them feel more comfortable and daring in their approaches to armed groups and to the conflict. By their very presence, CPT teams validate the dignity of Colombia's marginalized peoples. This validation encourages people to give the best of themselves, rather than giving up, joining armed groups, or displacing. Because of the reporting aspect of accompaniment, CPT's presence has helped to diminish the activities of armed groups and thus to open up the space for community organizing, dialogue, and economic development. The particular spirituality of CPT, which is a spirituality of ecumenism, of nonviolence, and of upholding the dignity of the human person, is seen as particularly valuable by some important leaders.

What has also become very clear throughout this investigation is the importance of the collaboration between CPT and *Programa*. CPT does not arrive in these communities alone or merely through its own decision-making process. CPT arrives by invitation, in order to support the life-sustaining projects developed by the community itself. CPT is not setting the agenda; the agenda is set by the communities, in collaboration with *Programa*, a highly trusted organization. If we are to understand CPT's work as mission, then, we will need to understand it as a paradigm of mission very different from its colonial, hegemonic past. CPT's way of doing mission takes the lead from local actors, especially local church actors.

We turn now to an examination of current trends in the theology of Christian mission. This theology seeks a praxis that the work of CPT fits into very well.

3

Constructing a New Mission Paradigm

The church does not have a mission, but the mission has a church.

—STEPHEN BEVANS AND ROGER SCHROEDER

UNTIL THE SIXTEENTH CENTURY, the term "mission" was used exclusively to describe the activity of the Trinity: the Father sending the Son and, in the common Western understanding, the Father and Son sending the Holy Spirit. The Jesuits began using the term in the sixteenth century to signify carrying out the tasks of the Pope, and specifically to spreading the Christian faith to those who were not Roman Catholic. In this way, the term became associated with the colonial expansion of the Western world, because that expansion involved the conquest of areas that were not previously Christian. In the twentieth century, in the wake of inde pendence movements and turmoil following World War II, the meaning of the term began changing again. This chapter attempts to trace, in very broad strokes, both change and continuity in approaches to mission since the time of Jesus. It does not attempt to cover all of Christian history, but only to look at key moments that have led to new approaches to mission in our own time. It then describes contemporary approaches to the theology and practice of mission, and suggests that when taken together, these ap proaches are best described using the metaphor of *accompaniment*.

The analysis uses three primary texts plus a large volume of supple mentary material. The primary texts are: David Bosch's *Transforming Mission: Paradigm Shifts in Theology of Mission*; Stephen Bevans and Roger Schroeder's *Constants in Context: A Theology of Mission for Today* and Paulo Suess' *Evangelizar desde los proyectos históricos de los otros*

Transforming Mission is a classic text in world mission studies, written by a South African Protestant theologian. Building on the work of Bosch, Catholic theologians Bevans and Schroeder propose a contemporary theology of mission in light of historical trends. Paulo Suess, one of the most respected Latin American missiologists, provides a corrective and critique of mission theologies originating from the perspective of former colonizing countries. Suess writes in Spanish, and all translations are mine.

CHRISTIAN MISSION IN HISTORICAL PERSPECTIVE

New Testament Roots

Although the concept of mission as it is currently understood only emerged in the latter part of the sixteenth century, it has rightly been said that the entire New Testament was written as a reflection on the early church's experiences with mission.[1] David Bosch reminds us that "the study of mission may be described as relating the always-relevant Jesus event of twenty centuries ago to the future of God's promised Reign by means of meaningful initiatives for the here and now."[2] We cannot reflect on contemporary mission without a return to the history, person, and ministry of Jesus, through whom God is revealed to us, and the experiences of the earliest apostles.

Bosch summarizes the missionary practice of Jesus and the early church:[3]

- It involved the person of Jesus himself, who shocked his contemporaries because he did not fit into the set formulas of the time.

- It was political, and even revolutionary. Rather than divorcing the physical from the spiritual, Jesus preached that the Reign of God is ushered into the here and now.

- Its revolutionary nature was manifested through new relationships. No longer were there divisions between Jew and Greek, free and slave, rich and poor, woman and man. Further, early Christians

---

1. Bevans, "Themes and Questions in Missiology Today," 1 (quoting Martin Kahler).

2. Bosch, *Transforming Mission*, 24.

3. Ibid., 47–50.

were involved in ministry to the most marginalized of their time, the "poor, orphans, widows, mine-workers, prisoners, slaves, and travelers."[4]

- Early Christian mission did not heal or liberate everyone; rather it expressed a hope that had not yet been fulfilled. The Reign of God had been ushered in, but not fully completed.

- Jesus ministered in weakness, and out of that weakness was derived his strength. Thus, self-sacrifice, even martyrdom, and mission be long together.

Brazilian theologian Paulo Suess makes an important contribution to Bosch's summary by reminding us that the mission of Jesus was not concerned with constructing buildings.

> He sent his disciples as bearers of peace, stripped of power, without gold or scepter, wise as serpents and innocent as doves. In the Palestine of Jesus—and this is not just a cultural or historical fact, but a marker for evangelism—the grounding for mission was not to have one's own home; rather it was the gratuity of lodging in the homes of others and discovering the Easter experience while on the journey.[5]

It is only in the later work of the evangelists that we find the construction of geographically based communities.

The first evangelists expanded and built on Jesus' approach to mission. For Matthew, mission involved the making of disciples who would practice God's call to justice and love. Those disciples should be formed into communities who seek to live out the teachings of Jesus together. This involves making new believers who are "sensitive to the needs of others, opening their eyes and hearts to recognize injustice, suffering, oppression, and the plight of those who have fallen by the wayside."[6]

Bosch's analysis illustrates that Luke-Acts provides a more complex mission paradigm that builds upon and expands the thinking found in Matthew.

---

4. Ibid., 49.

5. Suess, *Evangelizer desde los proyectos historicos de los otros*, 6.

6. Bosch, *Transforming Mission*, 81.

- Mission is understood as "witness," meaning proclamation that the "good news of the reign of God is Jesus Christ, incarnated, crucified, and risen, and what he has accomplished."[7]

- The witness of the missionaries "aims at repentance and forgiveness, which leads to salvation."[8] Conversion, then, implies a radical change of life that comes with the moral obligation to act in a Christian manner.

- Luke pays special attention to salvation as constituting economic justice for the poor.

- Peacemaking—nonviolent resistance to evil and to the destructive nature of hatred and vengeance—is intrinsic to the missionary message.

- The community of believers has an inward focus on prayer, teaching, and fellowship, and an outward focus on the salvation of those still outside of the community.

- Mission by its very nature encounters adversity and suffering, and parallels Jesus' journey to Jerusalem.

Through his deep engagement in mission, meaning the formation of Christian communities outside of Jerusalem, Paul also develops a comprehensive theology of mission.[9] He envisions a world marked by Christian unity. Once a person is baptized, there is no longer any room for religious, gender, ethnic, or class divisions. "Any form of segregation in the church, whether racial, ethnic, social, or whatever, is in Paul's understanding a denial of the Gospel."[10] Churches marked by the unity of the body of Christ are what should come into existence as a result of mission work.

Paul's apocalyptic theology rejects any notion of complete non-involvement in the world. "Because of God's sure victory in the end Paul emphasizes not ethical passivity but active participation in God's redemptive will in the here and now."[11] However, Christian ethics are based not on an objective knowledge of what is good, but rather on knowing that Christ is Lord, and therefore on serving Christ. The Christian must have a dual orientation: we must serve Christ through serving one another, thereby

7. Ibid., 116.
8. Ibid., 117.
9. Ibid., 171–78.
10. Ibid., 172.
11. Ibid., 176.

erecting signs of God's Reign in the here and now, and at the same time we must not fall into the trap of believing that through our own efforts the Reign of God will come about. We participate in God's redemptive activ ity, but we do not cause it.

Christian active engagement with the world will, by its very nature, involve suffering, weakness, and even death. This the Christian missionary gladly suffers for the sake of the salvation of the world. In other words, Christian mission is not for the sake of the church itself; it is done for the sake of the redemption of the world. "In Christ, God has reconciled not only to the church, but the world to himself."[12]

In short, early Christian mission involved creating new Christian communities, within the old world, that witnessed to a radically new kind of relationship: one based on a shared identity in Christ, on economic justice, and on peace through repentance, forgiveness, and reconciliation. These churches were to be signs of the coming Reign of God, which ulti mately cannot be ushered in through human hands, but only at the initia tive of God. Becoming a sign of the coming Reign by its very nature will involve suffering and death, and this fate the Christian accepts, not for the sake of an institutional church, but in order to bring about God's Reign.

From the New Testament to the Colonial Period[13]

Thanks to the work of Paul and subsequent missionaries, by the begin ning of the fourth century Christians comprised about 10 percent of the population of the Roman Empire. At the end of the third century, the Ro man Emperor launched an empire-wide persecution against the Christian threat to Roman traditional religious practices. However, Christian con versions continued unabated, and by the year 313 Emperor Constantine legalized Christianity. In 381 Emperor Theodosius made Christianity the official state religion. Prior to 313, membership in the Christian commu nity involved the possibility of violent martyrdom; after Constantine it became advantageous to be Christian.

In this context the practice of monasticism developed. A kind of martyrdom of asceticism replaced the martyrdom of torture and death for men and women who chose the monastic life. Some monks led the life of hermits, but others travelled the countryside preaching the Gospel. Com munities of monks formed, and many were sought after for their spiritual

12. Ibid., 178.
13. This section draws from Bevans, "Short History of Mission."

wisdom. Monasticism became a powerful agent of Christian evangelization, and remains so today.

Around the thirteenth century the mendicant movement arose, and it became the primary way the Gospel was preached until the sixteenth century. The best-known examples of this were the Franciscans and the Dominicans. They came into being in the context of widespread church corruption and excessive power. The mendicant movements called for a return to simplicity, preaching, and witness to the Gospel.

The Colonial Distortion

At the end of the fifteenth century, an agricultural economy controlled by fragmented feudal lords in Medieval Europe was being replaced by absolute monarchies that were overtaking the power that the church once held. At the same time, scientific discoveries made it possible to explore the oceans, and in 1492, Columbus crossed the Atlantic and discovered what was for Europe the "New World." Soldiers, settlers, and religious missionaries soon followed. Spain, Portugal, England, France, and others began to exploit the Americas for its natural resources and vast expanses of land. Earnings were sent back to enrich the European crowns.

Contrary to common rhetoric, there was nothing about the Americas that was "new" or "discovered" by the Europeans. The European conquest was a foreign intervention into the history of indigenous peoples whose history began 40,000 years prior with migrations from Asia. The indigenous peoples of what is now called the Americas—perhaps 90 million strong[14]—together comprised an enormous cultural richness and diversity.

> This diversity and richness was expressed in their monuments, pyramids, sculpture, mythology, medicine, and social organization. We also have massive literary documents, such as the Popol Vuh, Chilam Balam, Remembrance of Solola, and other indigenous chronicles, which portray the spiritual richness of the indigenous peoples, before and after the so-called discovery.[15]

Conquering the indigenous peoples became part of the European project, and today estimates vary widely as to how many were killed, but

14. Suess, 18.
15. Ibid., 19–20.

perhaps as many as 60 million perished through war, famine, or disease. On several of the Caribbean islands, the indigenous were completely wiped out within a century of Columbus's landing. In other places, nothing but a remnant was left. In present-day Colombia, as noted earlier, the indigenous make up less than five percent of the population today. In other countries such as Bolivia, Peru, and Guatemala, indigenous populations make up a majority or near-majority of the population, but they have long lacked political or economic power. In the United States, after the slaughter of the Indian Wars, the indigenous survivors were forced onto reservations, the majority of which were made up of unproductive lands that the European settlers did not want.

The enslavement of Africans was another feature of the European conquest. This was nothing new, but after Europeans settled the Americas, it took on a new intensity, as African slaves were increasingly used for hard labor, to replace the rapidly diminishing numbers of indigenous peoples. It is estimated that "over a four-hundred-year period, ten to twelve million Africans were transported to the 'New World,' another one or two million died in the 'middle passage' across the Atlantic, and possibly twelve million more died during the march from inland Africa before even reaching the holding areas on the coast."[17] The brutality of slavery ensured its continuation. African slaves were used to work plantations and mines. Many died as a result of hard labor and were replaced by new slaves taken from Africa.

The fifteenth century found Spain and Portugal quarreling over the right to control and exploit the new lands. In that context,

> the pope drew a line from the North Pole to the South Pole, separating the two domains. Furthermore, he created a *patronatus* system, giving the royal leaders of those two countries the rights and responsibilities for the missionary task. Under such a theocratic mentality, the official goals of the conquest were linked: to annex the conquered lands and to incorporate the baptized people into the Catholic Church.[18]

The Spanish established the *encomienda* system in its colonies, which meant that indigenous peoples were put under the charge of the Spanish settlements. The settlers had the right to exploit the labor of indigenous people, and the responsibility to teach them the Christian faith and baptize

16. Bevans and Schroeder, *Constants in Context*, 175.

17. Ibid., 172–73.

18. Ibid., 174.

them. The French and Portuguese also required that their slaves, both indigenous and African, be baptized. The theological motivation for this was that the majority of theologians believed that there was no salvation outside the church. In other words, although there were exceptions, most missionaries believed that forced baptism was necessary to guarantee an afterlife for their slaves. But, as Bosch points out, there was also a cultural motivation. Christians believed in the superiority of their religion, and because religion is deeply entwined with culture, this feeling of superiority also manifested in their sense of cultural superiority over non-European peoples. They believed this: "Just as the West's religion was predestined to be spread around the globe, the West's culture was to be victorious over all others."[19]

Further, the sixteenth century saw the birth and development of the ideology of race, which settlers and missionaries alike used as justification for the exploitation, enslavement, and murder of indigenous peoples and Africans. Anthropologist Audrey Smedley describes race as a "folk classification" that evolved from the sixteenth through the nineteenth centuries as a product of popular beliefs about human differences that appeared as a result of the experiences of European peoples and nations that had become expansionist, conquering, and dominating on a worldwide scale.[20] Elements of the ideology of race did not exist in the Old World, and from earliest times the peoples of the Nile, the Mediterranean, the Arabian Peninsula, southern Europe, and Africa visited one another, traded, warred, and made alliances without referring to race. From the written record we know that variations in physical features were rarely commented on. Think, for example, of the Biblical record. What the Bible recognized were ethnic differences, or those differences displayed by clusters of people living in specific areas who developed cultural, linguistic, or lifestyle traits particular to their group.

Race as a category did not originate as a product of scientific investigations and initially had no basis in the scientific studies of the times. Beginning in the mid- to late eighteenth century, scientists undertook to document the existence of racial differences that the European worldview had created and therefore demanded.[21] Race was a way of categorizing what were already perceived as unequal populations. Had the European

19. Bosch, *Transforming Mission*, 292.
20. Smedley, *Race in North America*, 25.
21. Ibid., 26.

explorers considered all human beings inherently equal, there would have been no need for racial categories.

Race became a new mode of human identification that superseded kinship, ethnicity, place of origin, religion, or any of the other features that had historically been used to differentiate peoples. Race was said to rest on physical characteristics, but in fact was fabricated out of the need to subjugate conquered peoples, and then with time was internalized as the principal form of human identity.[22] By the early nineteenth century, race had taken on the character of an ideology with an underlying basis in theology: Each group was created this way by God, so differences were fixed and unalterable.[23]

Inequality was a central component of race ideology, and was deemed ordained by God and part of natural law. During this same pe riod science began to confirm the inequalities. Scientific studies began to systematically measure and describe differences in hair texture, skin color, average height, and cranial size in various races, reflecting an assumption that the world had an intrinsically hierarchical order. At the same time anthropologists testified to evidence of cultural, social, spiritual, and tech nological inferiority throughout history.[24] Thus, indigenous peoples and Africans were baptized in order to ensure their salvation, and exploited for their labor, because it was thought that they were savages and not capable of anything more in their short life on Earth, made even shorter by the brutality of slavery. Today scholars understand that the indigenous and Africans came from highly developed and complex cultures with unique languages, ethnicities, geographic locations, religious traditions, and so cial structures. Their cultures were different from the European, but dif ferent does not mean inferior—it just means different.

Christian missionaries for the most part subscribed to the European worldview and worked within the official state concept of mission. There were, of course, exceptions. Dominicans, Franciscans, Jesuits, and Augus tinians all brought more communal models of mission to the "New World" that did not involve the same degree of cruelty. Many of these missionaries attempted to keep their distance from the conquest, and developed what they called *conventos*: small communities with a few Spanish families and hundreds of indigenous, and that might include a church, hospital, school, and orphanage. Made famous in the movie *The Mission*, the Jesuits also

22. Ibid., 338.
23. Ibid., 28.
24. Wander et al., "Roots of Racial Classification," 30.

developed settlements, or *reducciones*, where the indigenous would be protected from the worst aspects of the conquest.[25]

The most famous spokesperson for this worldview was Bartolome de las Casas, a Spanish Dominican who spoke out strongly against the conquest and its treatment of native peoples. He became known as the "Defender of the Indians." Theologian Justo Gonzalez calls Bartolome de las Casas and other dissenters "voices of compassion": missionaries who defied the prevailing worldview and developed a theological outlook based on their experiences in the mission lands. Far from being an isolated voice, Gonzalez depicts Bartolome de las Casas as being part of an organized movement that sought political and structural alternatives to the Spanish conquest. Gonzalez emphasizes, however, that in bringing to light the compassion of these missionaries, he has no desire to minimize the effects of the conquest.

> On the contrary, I am convinced that the so-called "encounter" between two hemispheres led to one of the greatest tragedies in human history, and one of the worst blots on Christian history. The death of millions upon millions of human beings, the disappearance of entire civilizations and peoples, and the subjugation of others for 500 years should not be obscured nor minimized. The cries of trampled and destroyed generations still rise to heaven, and justice still remains to be done.[26]

In other words, these efforts were the exceptions, and even with these more humane models of mission, and among the most enlightened of missionaries, the prevailing worldview was one of the superiority of the Christian religion, of European culture, and of the so-called white race.

The Western supremacist worldview became even more pronounced in the latter part of the nineteenth century, an era known as the "heyday of colonialism."[27] During this period Western mission work became entwined with "manifest destiny." Manifest destiny, a product of nationalism, was the notion that not only was Western culture and religion superior to all others, but that God had chosen the Western nations to spread this culture and religion to the ends of the earth. Thus, "virtually every white nation regarded itself as being chosen for a particular destiny and as having a unique charisma: the Germans, the French, the Russians, the British,

---

25. Bevans and Schroeder, *Constants in Context*, 176–83.

26. Gonzalez, *Voices of Compassion*, 163.

27. Bosch, *Transforming Mission*, 298.

the Americans, the Afrikaners, the Dutch."[28] This nationalism translated into missionary zeal, and "civilization" through conformity to Western culture and the spreading of the Gospel were seen as two sides of the same coin.[29] Nearly all missionaries were operating from an assumption of their own superiority.

There were, of course, exceptions to the prevailing missionary practice.

> A few missionaries were against imposing Western culture; many missionaries defended the interests and dignity of the colonized peoples; and others understood their efforts as a positive response to past sins of the West, particularly regarding its part in the slave trade.[30]

Furthermore, it would be a mistake to simply characterize the Western missionary endeavor as a one-sided imposition of Western values and culture with no positive aspects. The peoples who were on the receiving end of missionary work were not just passive recipients. There are numerous examples of indigenous peoples incorporating Christianity and Western culture into their own worlds, creating unique Christian cultures that made sense within their own values and traditions.

But the exceptions, as well as the efforts of indigenous peoples to cope with the conquest, do not erase the picture of violence, forced labor, genocide, and cultural destruction that took place on a massive scale during the colonial period. Missionaries, even those who tried to mitigate colonialism's negative effects, for the most part did not doubt the legitimacy of the colonial project.

Twentieth-Century Uncertainties

The beginning of the twentieth century, despite the interruption of World War I, saw a continuation of nineteenth-century models, which "understood mission primarily in terms of the extension of the church—extension either by the conversion of individuals, or by the establishment of ecclesiastical structures in non-Christian territories."[31] With the end of colonization and the rise of independence movements, which happened

---

28. Ibid., 299.
29. Bevans and Schroeder, *Constants in Context*, 231.
30. Ibid., 231.
31. Bevans and Schroeder, *Constants in Context*, 281.

primarily in the 1940s through the 1970s, as well as the turmoil of the 1960s, many missionaries began to doubt the legitimacy of their project, and mission groups began to understand the need to respect the dignity of local cultures, identities, and religious traditions. This uncertainty led to a dramatic decline in the number of missionaries after 1968. "Among Protestants and Catholics alike, the very idea of mission activity—and foreign missionary activity in particular—was being called into question,"[32] and some prominent missionaries called for an end to missionary activity altogether.

Catholic theologian Robert Schreiter divides the twentieth and early twenty-first century into four periods: certainty (1919–1962); ferment (1962–1965); crisis (1965–1975); and rebirth (1975 to present).[33] The period of certainty is characterized by the optimism present during the late nineteenth century, but also by the beginning of reflection about the missionary endeavor by the missionaries themselves. The period of ferment was the time of the Second Vatican Council, when the document *Ad Gentes* was promulgated. This document and others marked a dramatic shift in Catholic understandings of church, and therefore mission. After the Council, during the period of crisis, missionaries began to grasp the full implications of the documents and the new approach, and their numbers declined. The fourth period, the period of rebirth, is marked by the development of new theologies and forms of mission activity, and begins with the publication of Pope Paul VI's document *Evangelii Nuntiandi*. We are still in the period of rebirth, and my analysis and investigation can be considered part of the conversation about the future of mission.

Some have suggested that the entire missionary endeavor is a child of the Enlightenment and Western expansion, and as the world moves beyond Enlightenment thinking, we should also move beyond missionary thinking. Most Christians, however, would argue that Christianity is missionary by its very nature, and that it is possible to salvage the missionary project by moving to a new paradigm of mission that is not intrinsically hegemonic or supremacist, which is my position. We turn now to looking at later twentieth-century theologies of mission that attempt to move us to a new paradigm in a changing world.

32. Bevans and Gros, *Evangelization and Religious Freedom*, 60.
33. Schreiter, "Changes in Roman Catholic Attitudes," 113–25.

CONTEMPORARY THEOLOGIES OF MISSION

David Bosch: An Ecumenical Missionary Paradigm

David Bosch argues that, as a result of shifting worldviews in the wake of the failures of Enlightenment thinking, Christianity is undergoing a major paradigm shift in its approach to mission. A paradigm shift does not mean that the churches should take a reactionary or strictly revolutionary approach to mission in the new millennium. Rather, it points to continuity with the past, and at the same time changing past practices, leading to a kind of creative tension between tradition and transformation.

Foundational to this paradigm shift is a new approach to ecclesiology. Stated very simply, Protestants and Catholics alike have shifted from "an emphasis on a church-centered mission to a mission-centered church." What this means practically is that the primary focus of mission is no longer the establishment of new churches (complete with buildings) in the mission lands. Instead, the missionary task defines the nature of the church. Thus, in response to questions about why send missionaries at all in light of the abuses, the church answers that we are inherently missionary: we are sent to proclaim the Reign of God.

The question then becomes: What does missionary activity look like in this changing ecclesiology? Bosch, relying heavily on New Testament approaches to mission, spells out its dimensions. First, in a new and globalized world, emphasis is placed on the unity of the Body of Christ. There cannot be a dichotomy between doctrinal truth and Christian unity; Christian unity as preached by Paul is the supreme Gospel value. Thus, a new missionary paradigm must be ecumenical in nature.

Second, ecumenism does not mean that we erase differences. Unity and difference must exist in tension with one another. This tension, Bosch says, calls us to repentance. "Ecumenism is only possible where people accept each other despite differences. Our goal is not a fellowship exempt from conflict, but one which is characterized by unity in reconciled diversity . . . The post-modern paradigm manifests itself as unity which preserves diversity and diversity which strives after unity."[35]

Third, the world can no longer be divided into "sending churches" and "mission field." The missionary task will never be completed and the mission field is everywhere. All people are always on a journey of faith,

34. Bosch, *Transforming Mission*, 370.
35. Ibid., 465.

which does not come to an end at some point of perfection in the future. Further, the distinction between sending and receiving churches no longer exists. A new paradigm of mission calls for "new relationships, mutual responsibility, accountability, and interdependence (not independence!)—not just because . . . the West's dominance, numerically and otherwise, appears to have ended definitely, but rather because there can be no 'higher' or 'lower' in the Body of Christ."[36]

If we are to emphasize unity, and thus the one mission of the one church, then the new paradigm must take a stand against the "proliferation of new churches" in places where Christian churches already exist. Planting new churches focuses on difference rather than unity. Paul sought to build communities that would deal with all of their economic, social, cultural, and religious differences, learning to love one another and worship together. Instead of planting new churches, Christians of all varieties should come together under one roof.

The purpose of mission is not to serve the institutional church. The purpose of mission is to serve humanity, and the church serves the mission. The Reign of God is a vision of a unified humanity, and the church is called to be a prophetic sign of that promised Reign. Furthermore, Christian churches must become the Reign of God if we are to preach it to the world. The loss of ecclesial unity is a sin, because it is contrary to the unity envisioned in God's future promise for the world. In other words, the purpose of mission is not for the sake of building up any individual church or denomination; rather, it is to do God's work in bringing about God's future Reign. An invitation to join the church is done not for the sake of the church but for the sake of God's Reign.

Bosch's new paradigm for mission answers a number of the questions raised in response to past missionary excesses and is a powerful statement about the purpose of the church. We are not meant to be self-serving; we are meant to serve humanity. However many would argue, including me, that an ecumenical paradigm does not go far enough in describing the nature of the Reign of God that we are proclaiming, and that Bosch's analysis was a strong beginning to a conversation that continues. In the following sections we turn to some additional theological approaches that emerged in the latter part of the twentieth century, but we will return to Bosch's ecumenical paradigm later in this chapter.

36. Ibid., 466.

Papal Documents: Ad Gentes, Evangelii Nuntiandi, and Redemptoris Missio

Decree Ad Gentes on the Missionary Activity of the Church was approved in 1965 by the Second Vatican Council and was the first Roman Catholic encyclical to take up the matter of the *theology* of mission. Seeming to agree with Bosch's conclusions, *Ad Gentes* begins by answering unequivocally that the need for mission work is urgent as never before, and that the purpose of mission is to "spread the reign of Christ" everywhere.[37] Further, *Ad Gentes* is most famous for the first line of the second paragraph: "the pilgrim Church is missionary by her very nature."[38]

Fundamentally, *Ad Gentes* views the church is missionary by nature because God is missionary by nature. The Trinitarian God is an overflowing of love through Christ and the Holy Spirit, and the church was formed through that love. In the practice of mission, however, *Ad Gentes* was trying to deal with two opposing positions of what mission was supposed to *do* that had developed in the early twentieth century. Those positions were, on the one hand, that mission should focus on preaching the gospel, through word and through deed, and individual conversion; and on the other hand, that mission should focus on planting churches, and thus on developing buildings and a hierarchy of clergy and bishops to go with them. The document accepts both ideas: mission continues to be understood in terms of territory, but is also understood in terms of outreach to individual persons.

Ad Gentes does recognize that in planting new churches there is a need to respect local cultures and contexts, and to adapt local traditions into the new Christian churches:

> (The new churches) . . . borrow from the customs and traditions of their people, from their wisdom and their learning, from their arts and disciplines, all those things which can contribute to the glory of their Creator, or enhance the grace of their Savior, or dispose Christian life the way it should be.[39]

Ad Gentes does not discuss the work of justice and peace as an element of mission. Vatican II dealt with those issues more comprehensively in a different document: *Gaudium et Spes*. However, mission as described in *Ad Gentes* and the work of justice and peace as described in *Gaudium*

---

37. *Ad Gentes* 1.
38. Ibid., 2.
39. *Ad Gentes* 22.

et Spes become more closely tied in later mission documents, especially *Evangelii Nuntiandi*, an apostolic exhortation published by Pope Paul VI in 1975. With this document, the missionary movement "came to a new understanding and a new birth."[40]

In 1974 Pope Paul VI convened a Synod of Bishops to address the topic "Evangelization in the Modern World." The bishops were not able to agree on a final document, and so requested that Pope Paul VI use their material to write his own, and this formed the basis for *Evangelii Nuntiandi*. Pope Paul reaffirms the inherent missionary nature of the church, pointing to its origins in the evangelizing activity of Jesus and the apostles.[41] However, Pope Paul moves away from the Trinitarian approach to mission found in *Ad Gentes* and instead focuses on Jesus' work as an evangelizer proclaiming the Reign of God, which is the key to salvation. Salvation involves liberation "from everything that oppresses."[42] Indeed, from the beginning the apostles were witnessing to the rest of the world what they had seen and experienced in Jesus' life, death, and resurrection. Their witness took the form of communal life, prayer, preaching, and the sharing of worldly goods, and as a result of their witness, many were baptized.[43] "Mission, in other words, is what it means to be church, because to be church means to share in the mission of Jesus, which was to preach, to serve and to witness with his whole heart to the kingdom of God."[44]

Pope Paul significantly expanded the understanding of what missionaries *do*. He cautioned against any "partial or fragmentary" conception of evangelization, and pointed to several documents of Vatican II, *Gaudium et Spes*, *Ad Gentes*, and *Lumen Gentium*, as containing the essential elements of mission activity,[45] which include the following:

- The Gospel is proclaimed above all by witness. Witness refers to the "sharing of life and destiny with other people, (and) . . . solidarity with the efforts of all for whatever is noble and good." It involves presence and sharing, and is the first and essential element in evangelization.[46]

- Witness alone is insufficient. Witness must be "made explicit by a clear and unequivocal proclamation of the Lord Jesus. The Good

---

40. Bevans and Gros, *Evangelization and Religious Freedom*, 61–62.

41. Pope Paul VI, *Evangelii Nuntiandi*, 14–15.

42. Ibid., 9.

43. Acts 2:41–47.

44. Bevans and Schroeder, *Constants in Context*, 306.

45. Pope Paul VI, *Evangelii Nuntiandi*, 17.

46. Ibid., 21.

News proclaimed by the witness of life sooner or later has to be pro claimed by the word of life."[47]

- Witness and proclamation should lead to adherence to "the new manner of being, of living . . . which the Gospel inaugurates." Thus, witness and proclamation lead to a transformation based on Gospel values.[48]

- This change of life is revealed concretely by "a visible entry into a community of believers. Thus those whose life has been transformed enter a community which is itself a sign of transformation."[49]

- The person who is evangelized goes on to evangelize others.[50]

- Proclamation includes a variety of elements: hope in God's prom ised future for humanity; love for all; the human capacity of giving and forgiving, which spring from the love of God; and includes an explicit message about "the rights and duties of every human being, about family life . . . , about life in society, about international life, peace, justice and development."[51]

Evangelii Nuntiandi thus envisions a three-stage process of evangeli zation: Christian witness, leading to transformation, which includes join ing a faith community, and leading to evangelization of others. Pope Paul's exhortation broke new ground in the church's thinking about mission, and "demonstrated the comprehensiveness of the church's evangelizing mis sion and its continuing relevance in a world not only of newly indepen dent nations, newly appreciated cultures, and newly revived religions, but also of struggle, violence, and institutionalized structures of poverty and oppression."[52]

To commemorate the 25th anniversary of *Ad Gentes*, in 1990 John Paul II issued a new encyclical on mission, *Redemptoris Missio* which further developed the Catholic understanding of mission. While affirming the theologies of mission outlined in *Ad Gentes* and *Evangelii Nuntiandi*, John Paul II answers the question *Why mission?* somewhat dif ferently. The church is missionary by nature because Jesus is the "definitive

47. Ibid., 22.
48. Ibid., 23.
49. Ibid.
50. Ibid., 24.
51. Ibid., 28–29.
52. Bevans and Gros, *Evangelization and Religious Freedom*, 65.

self-revelation of God."[53] Because one comes to communion with God only through the mediation of Jesus, it is therefore the function of the church to proclaim this truth to everyone. In short, the encyclical involves an emphasis on the risen Christ, instead of the life and ministry of Jesus (*Evangelii Nuntiandi*), or of God as relational outpouring of love (*Ad Gentes*).

In answer to the question of what missionaries *do*, Pope John Paul states that "missionary activity proper" still involves proclaiming the Christian gospel, building up the local church, and promulgating Christian values to non-Christians.[54] He distinguishes between two areas of mission: "missionary activity proper" and "new evangelization." New evangelization is a reference to Pope Paul VI's definition of mission as evangelization in *Evangelii Nuntiandi*, which refers to what missionaries do in a context that is already Christian but in need of a renewal. The renewal would then involve Pope Paul's threefold process, whereas missionary activity proper would involve the long-established activities of building up churches. However, he says that the boundaries between the two areas of mission are not actually that clear, and they should not be placed into "watertight compartments."[55]

John Paul II offers concrete "paths" by which missionary activity is developed: witness, proclamation, forming new churches, ecumenism, inculturation, interreligious dialogue, working for development and liberation, and charitable works.

- **Witness**. "The missionary who, despite all his or her human limitations and defects, lives a simple life, taking Christ as the model, is a sign of God and of transcendent realities." This involves concern for people, charity, and work for justice, peace, and human rights.[56] It also involves taking "courageous and prophetic stands in the face of the corruption of political or economic power."[57]

- **Proclamation**. "Proclamation is the permanent priority of mission . . . The subject of proclamation is Christ who was crucified, died and is risen: through him is accomplished our full and authentic liberation from evil, sin and death; through him God bestows "new life"

---

53. Pope John Paul II, *Redemptoris Missio*, 5.
54. Ibid., 34.
55. Ibid.
56. Ibid., 42.
57. Ibid., 43.

that is divine and eternal."[58] The aim of proclamation is Christian conversion.[59]

- **Forming New Churches.** "The mission *ad gentes* has this objective: to found Christian communities and develop churches to their full maturity. This is a central and determining goal of missionary activity, so much so that the mission is not completed until it succeeds in building a new particular church which functions normally in its local setting."[60]

- **Ecumenism.** "It is thus urgent to work for the unity of Christians, so that missionary activity can be more effective. At the same time we must not forget that efforts toward unity are themselves a sign of the work of reconciliation which God is bringing about in our midst."

- **Inculturation.** The church makes the Gospel incarnate in different cultures and at the same time introduces peoples, together with their cultures, into the Christian community. In this way both the practice of Christianity and the local culture are transformed. Through inculturation the Church becomes "a more effective instrument of mission."[62] Missionaries must immerse themselves in the local culture and learn the local language, thus discovering the value of the culture through their own experience in it.[63]

- **Interreligious Dialogue.** There is no conflict between proclaiming Christ and engaging in dialogue with non-Christian faiths. Both are proper to the missionary vocation, but they "should not be regarded as interchangeable."[64] Dialogue seeks the "elimination of prejudice, intolerance, and misunderstandings."[65]

- **Development and Liberation.** Human development comes primarily not from material assistance, but from "formation of consciences" and "maturing of ways of thinking and patterns of behavior."[66] "fosters the recognition of each person's dignity, encourages solidar

58. Ibid., 44.
59. Ibid., 46.
60. Ibid., 48.
61. Ibid., 50.
62. Ibid., 52.
63. Ibid., 53.
64. Ibid., 55.
65. Ibid., 56.
66. Ibid., 57.

ity, commitment and service of one's neighbor, and gives everyone a place in God's plan, which is the building of (the) kingdom of peace and justice."[67]

- **Charitable Works.** The church is called to be "on the side of those who are poor and oppressed in any way . . . Works of charity reveal the soul of all missionary activity: love, which has been and remains the driving force of mission."[68]

Redemptoris Missio affirms the emphasis on church-planting found in *Ad Gentes*, disregarding the cautions against a focus on church-planting that we find reflected in Bosch and that we will see in Suess. It also affirms Pope Paul's focus on witness through presence, solidarity, service, and working for human development and liberation. It also adds a new element: interreligious dialogue, which is to coexist alongside proclamation of Christ crucified and risen as the work of missionaries.

In these three major mission documents of the Catholic Church we see separate but overlapping theologies and separate but overlapping visions of the life and work of a missionary. However, these documents did not put an end to the questions about *why* we need missionaries and what missionaries should *do*. In fact, if anything, the questioning has intensified. Placing interreligious dialogue alongside proclamation raises the theological question of how to relate the aims of the two endeavors. How are we to understand the seemingly conflicting principles that salvation is to be found only through Jesus Christ, on the one hand, and that there are salvific elements in other religions, on the other? Approaching another religion with the former as our starting point would seem to doom the dialogue from the start.

Catholic theologian Robert Schreiter has suggested that "conversion to Christianity in any significant numbers is about to come to an end."[69] In today's world, the "religious geography" is more or less settled, and this reality would seem to render much less relevant the core activities of missionaries as outlined in *Ad Gentes* and *Redemptoris Missio*, and much more relevant the evangelization activities proposed by *Evangelii Nuntiandi*, which focus on those who are already Christian. Indeed, in October 2012 the Vatican launched its Year of Faith initiative for the Catholic

---

67. Ibid., 59.

68. Ibid., 60.

69. Schreiter, "Challenges Today to Mission 'Ad Gentes.'"

Church worldwide. Meant to be a tool for a "New Evangelization," its aim is precisely those Catholics who have fallen away from their faith.

Highlighting charitable works as the soul of missionary work, found in *Redemptoris Missio*, is also an issue for future inquiry. Charity can be, and frequently has been, nothing more than an extension of colonialism. In other words, the colonial, or dominant, power exploits the labor and thus profits from a given community, and then provides charity to help alleviate the poverty that the colonial power itself has created. Charity maintains the power differential between giver and receiver, may not ac knowledge the abilities of the receiver to act on his or her own behalf, and can foster a dependence that becomes difficult to overcome. We will discuss this issue further later in this chapter.

In the following section, we will look at how Bevans and Schroeder, in their book *Constants in Context*, strive to create a synthesis of the three strains of Catholic thinking found in the documents discussed above, as well as the thinking of David Bosch, and at the same time take into ac count a changed world environment in order to determine a single but coherent paradigm for mission.

Bevans and Schroeder: Mission as Prophetic Dialogue

We have seen that mission theology in the latter part of the twentieth century saw the development of three separate but related approaches: mission as participation in the life and mission of the Trinity; mission as continuation of the life's work of Jesus to preach, teach, and witness to the Reign of God; and mission as proclamation of the risen Christ as unique savior of the world. Bevans and Schroeder suggest that there are limitations to each of the approaches when taken alone, and only with a synthesis of all three will we have a comprehensive theology of mission for our time.

The danger in focusing on the central role of the Holy Spirit is that the central role of Christ might be eclipsed and this could lead to a denial of the uniqueness of Christ and of salvation through Christ.[70] The danger of focusing exclusively on mission as service to God's Reign is that it can lead to an understanding of mission as limited to human development work.[71] The danger of a strict focus on Christ as universal savior is that

---

70. Bevans and Schroeder, *Constants in Context*, 303–4.

71. Ibid., 321–22.

it can lead to a "spiritualizing" of conversion that ignores injustice and oppression.[72]

Bevans and Schroeder write eloquently of the need for a new approach:

> No longer can we conceive of mission in terms of church expansion or the salvation of souls; no longer can we conceive of mission as supporting the outreach of colonial powers; no longer can we understand missionary activity as providing the blessings of Western civilization to "underdeveloped" or "developing" peoples and cultures; no longer can we conceive of mission as originating from a Christianized North and moving toward a non-Christian or a religiously underdeveloped South. Mission today, rather, is something much more modest and at the same time much more exciting—and indeed more urgent.[73]

They propose that the starting point for such a model of mission today is *dialogue.*

Dialogue expresses the Trinitarian nature of God. "Just as God in Godself is a community of dialogue and acts for the salvation of the world in a non-coercive, persuasive manner, so must those baptized into this Trinitarian community act in mission."[74] Dialogue, as imitation of God, involves first a self-emptying that includes listening, learning, and relationship building. As such, it is first a ministry of presence. But dialogue must also be prophetic, and so the missionary must live in a community that expresses Christian values, convey an unshakeable commitment to justice, peace and the integrity of creation, and speak to the "truth of the Gospel and the person of Jesus Christ," proclaiming one's faith confidently to the world.[75] This paradigm of mission, which they call *prophetic dialogue,* brings together each of the theological concerns expressed by the papal documents and is meant to be a synthesis of the many proposals put forward by popes and theologians alike about what missionaries *do* in today's changed world.

The practice of *prophetic dialogue* is multifaceted, and Bevans and Schroeder name six elements: witness and proclamation; liturgy, prayer, and contemplation; commitment to justice, peace, and the integrity of

72. Ibid., 346–47.
73. Ibid., 284–85.
74. Bevans and Gros, *Evangelization and Religious Freedom*, 96.
75. Ibid., 96–97.

creation; the practice of interreligious dialogue; efforts of inculturation; and the ministry of reconciliation.[76]

- **Witness and Proclamation.** Witness involves expressing Christian values through one's life and deeds. Proclamation is the confident and faithful announcement of the Lordship of Jesus and the Gospel message, but in a way that is humble, respectful, and dialogical in nature. It is a conversation that begins with listening.

- **Liturgy, Prayer, and Contemplation.** Liturgy prepares and nourish es Christians for mission; it is also a place where witness and procla mation take place. Listening, appreciating, and relationship building are contemplative processes grounded in our relationship with God and foundational to mission in our time.

- **Justice, Peace, and Integrity of Creation.** Mission involves a com mitment to preaching, serving, and witnessing to the Reign of God that involves working for justice and peace, as well as for the future of the whole of creation. These activities can involve working for eco nomic and political liberation and human rights, peace activism, and working for ecological stability. The church speaks *for* the poor to the world's powers, but works toward empowering them to speak for themselves. This also involves solidarity with the poor by adopting a simple lifestyle and dependence on God.

- **The Practice of Interreligious Dialogue.** Interreligious dialogue is a constitutive element of Christian mission. It should be done in a spir it of mutuality, encouraging both sides to explore more deeply their own faith traditions. It should also be implemented with the convic tion that Jesus Christ is the one and unique savior of the world.

- **Efforts at Inculturation.** The local context and culture must be taken seriously in theology, liturgy, proclamation of the Gospel, and train ing for ministry. In this way there is an exchange: the local context of fers its culture and traditions that enrich the church, and the church offers the Gospel, which enriches the local context.

- **The Ministry of Reconciliation.** Extreme violence marks many mission contexts today; thus mission activity must include a com mitment to work for reconciliation among divided peoples. It must be practiced on four levels: personal healing, cultural restoration,

76. Ibid., 99; Bevans and Schroeder, *Constants in Context*, 348–95.

political reconciliation, and, for Catholics, working to heal divisions within the Catholic Church.

The paradigm of prophetic dialogue proposed by Bevans and Schroeder goes a long way toward advancing us to a model of mission that leaves behind its colonial past. In proposing that the starting point is dialogue, mission begins as a conversation, rather than an imposition, and considers the local context before diving into a project. However, we are still left with questions, concerns, and gaps. First, this paradigm does not answer the question posed in the previous section: How can we conceive of interreligious dialogue based on a mutual exchange of equals if the aim of Christians continues to be proclamation of the unique Lordship of Jesus Christ through whom salvation can be found? If Schreiter is correct, and the religious geography of the world has been mostly settled, then the purpose of interreligious dialogue really becomes a mutual exchange in order to further understanding and tolerance, reduce religious-based violence, and reach reconciliation.

This paradigm also does not deal with the issue of ecumenism and ecumenical action raised by Bosch and encouraged in all three papal documents discussed earlier. They mention ecumenism as an aspect of inculturation, but this is never really developed. They also talk about the need for reconciliation within the Catholic Church, but not among Christian churches.[77] Bosch makes the point that unity among believers is constitutive of the biblical image of the Reign of God that we are to be witnessing and proclaiming. This expression of unity would not only involve dialogue, but the prophetic act of forming communities together and acting as one Body of Christ. Further, as has been well-documented elsewhere, religious differences, including differences among Christians, can be used as an excuse for violence in contexts of conflict and division. An ecumenical witness, together with interreligious dialogue, is part of a ministry of reconciliation.

Finally, one is left with the sense, even with this groundbreaking work, that Christian mission is still primarily a project of outside missionaries, conceived by them and carried out by them. They will try to adapt their project to suit local context and culture, but this is only so that it will be received better. It is still fundamentally their project. Even the metaphor of prophetic dialogue can express this approach, because it assumes that missionaries from the outside enter a new situation wanting to communicate their perspective in order to somehow transform the context.

77. Ibid., 384; 392.

It still creates an "other" who is the object of mission. Although *prophetic dialogue* is a helpful metaphor, Bevans and Schroeder do not make wide use of the metaphors for mission most commonly found in the writings of formerly colonized peoples, such as solidarity, fellowship or companion ship, and accompaniment, all of which take seriously the agency of local people. They do mention, quoting Robert Schreiter, that solidarity and ac companiment marked mission in the twentieth century until 1989, which marks the beginning of globalism. However, they do not explain why glo balism would render outdated those terms, especially when the churches of formerly colonized peoples are still using them widely.[78]

Schreiter defines accompaniment as "walking side by side, rather than leading and following" and says that because no realistic alternative has emerged to neoliberal capitalism, these earlier theological responses, while still retaining some validity, needed to be reworked after the fall of the Berlin Wall in 1989.[79] However, as we will see, the Latin American churches are still using this metaphor, and they have reworked and ex panded the definition.

In the following section, Brazilian theologian Paulo Suess offers additional input to this approach, by proposing that Christian mission should involve a metaphor of *fellowship* which supports the life projects of the communities themselves, rather than the projects of the missionaries.

Paulo Suess: Mission as Supporting the Life Projects of "The Others"

Suess agrees that a mission crisis is taking place in the wake of the twen tieth-century recognition that evangelization happened together with the colonization and cultural destruction of native peoples. He presents three theological questions that must be answered by missionaries today. These questions largely coincide with questions asked by other theologians and presented above. But Suess offers answers to these questions from a South American perspective, thus seeking to transform the "swords of colonial ism into plows of liberation."[80]

First, is a missionary presence necessary for salvation? Missionar ies during the colonial period were convinced that making people accept Christianity amounted to rescuing them from the eternal fire. However,

---

78. Ibid., 389.

79. Schreiter, *New Catholicity*, 126–27.

80 Suess, *Evangelizar desde los proyectos históricos de los otros*, 81–89.

today we understand that, through Divine Providence, "the innocent and people of good will"[81] are saved. For this reason, many missionaries are asking themselves: If salvation exists outside of the church, what makes my presence necessary?

The answer, Suess says, lies in what he describes as *gift*. He uses the Spanish word *gratuidad*, which could be translated as *gratuity*, but what he really means is a gift offered freely, without any claim or obligation in return. The church needs to displace itself from its comfortable position so that it does not stagnate and eventually die. The church must place itself within new cultures and contexts in order to maintain its own health and vitality. In other words, the purpose of mission is not to save "the others" from eternal fire. The purpose of mission is to keep the church healthy. From this perspective, mission is not a favor the church offers to others; it is a favor that "the others" offer to the missionaries by receiving them as guests in their homes and thus maintaining the vitality of the church. In return, missionaries offer the grace of their faith in Jesus as a kind of free-will offering. This gratuitous gift of missionaries' faith, offered through their presence, is what will transform the world. In short, Suess skirts the theological problem of where salvation is found by asserting that Christian mission is not really about salvation, at least not in its traditional meaning of the avoidance of damnation.

Stephen Bevans echoes this sentiment, that the church must engage in mission in order to sustain itself, in a later, unpublished, paper:

> The church comes to be as the church engages in mission—as it crosses the boundary of Judaism to the Gentiles, and realizes that its mission is the very mission of God: to go into the world and be God's saving, healing, challenging presence. Thus, the act of going to new places is itself the act of sustaining the church.[82]

The second question takes up the legitimacy of the missionary project. Suess writes that indigenous peoples question the manner in which the Gospel was transmitted, because so little respect was given to their cultures and history. They ask, then: By what right do we impose the Gospel on them, and by what means? The reality is that missionaries "confused the Good News of the Gospel with the bad news of civilization."[83] What, then, is our guarantee that the current missionary project will not again impose, as Suess puts it, an "alien civilization?"

81. Ibid., 83.
82. Bevans, "Mission Has a Church," 5.
83. Suess, *Evangelizar desde los proyectos históricos de los otros*, 84.

Suess answers that the legitimacy of mission lies in the concept of *fraternidad*, a Spanish word that I translate as *fellowship*. Although *frater nidad* is more often translated as *fraternity*, in my view the English word *fraternity* does not really convey Suess' meaning. It could also be rendered as *companionship*. We Christians are not owners of the faith of others, he writes. We are brothers and sisters, and the task of the missionary church is to recuperate the natural Christian fellowship that was lost during the colonial project. Fellowship is the same as love, and love is manifested in the following ways:

- Love and fellowship confirm that everyone is an agent of mission and capable of serving the people of God.

- Fellowship involves the participation of all in both material and spir itual treasure.

- Fellowship is collective and is exercised within a community.

- Fellowship is inclined toward listening first. It is empathetic and is a practice of solidarity, meaning that the missionary "suffers with" the crucified peoples.

- Because fellowship involves solidarity, Christian mission based in fellowship remains with the people, accepting the consequences.

Suess writes that a missionary project grounded in these practices, and which does not seek political or religious power, will win over the confi dence of the people.

A third question arises from the mandate to take a "preferential op tion for the poor," articulated by the bishops of Latin American and the Caribbean in Medellin in 1968, and also reflected in the call for charity and development in *Redemptoris Missio*. Suess suggests that an option for the poor that involves evangelizing them from the perspective of the dom inant culture is still a colonial practice. He asks, "What is the relevance of the history of these peoples for the history of salvation that we are an nouncing? What is the importance of their cultures to the essence of our missionary intervention?"[84]

The poor should not be defined by their deprivation. The poor are also subjects of their own historical-cultural project, and carriers of their own ancestral values and traditions. Suess proposes a new approach to evangelization that goes beyond the previous definitions of inculturation and involves an evangelization that takes as its starting point the context,

84. Ibid.

culture and history of the peoples whom the missionaries have inserted themselves into. As we will see, Suess' critique also goes to the heart of the problem with the *Redemptoris Missio* approach to charity as the soul of missionary activity.

The fundamental task of the church, and thus of the missionary, Suess says, is to announce the Reign of God.[85] Both the Gospel message and individual cultures are projects for life, and they can be complementary. The poor of Latin America remain subjects of their own cultures, not objects of missionary projects, and people move forward with their own projects for life, even when their original culture has been mutilated or destroyed. Life continues, and upon their cultural ruins people will elaborate new projects of life and hope. A holistic, inculturated evangelization would demonstrate the relevance of the Gospel for the life projects of the cultures and contexts into which it is inserted. The Gospel itself is a project for life, and it can demonstrate its relevance through supporting the construction of justice and solidarity. Christians can provide a kind of proof of the Reign of God, which is defined as the fullness of life, through their works of justice, equality, liberty, and fellowship.[86]

Further, it is through one's own culture that projects of life are constructed; thus the Gospel as a project of life must reinforce local cultures, and not try to replace them with Western Christian values or symbols.

> To demonstrate and reinforce paths of life and peace through praxis in the middle of "the others," evangelizers respond to situations of death and desperation that all peoples experience in their concrete lives . . . In these struggles, an inculturated evangelization strengthens the identity of the poor and thus restores the disfigured face of Christ in them.[87]

There is a disconnect between a Gospel transmitted in European or North American cultural concepts, and the multicultural reality of Latin America. The Gospel should not identify itself with any one culture, but should live in each of them, respecting and preserving them, and believing in the future they have constructed for themselves.[88]

When facing the "historical and daily massacres of the poor, the excluded, and the 'others,' the pastoral and political task will be: to support their autonomy, protagonism, and participation in democratic processes;

85. Ibid., 177.
86. Ibid., 130–34.
87. Ibid., 145.
88. Ibid., 163; 168.

to fight for their rights, and for justice, ethics, and a society based on soli darity; to strengthen their cultural identity and subjectivity; to articulate structural changes to address the root causes of poverty and violence; to generate a passion for justice based on the hope of our faith as well as on the struggle for life among the poor, excluded, and marginalized."[89]

Suess' description of the nature of missionary activity described here does not necessarily replace the paradigm of prophetic dialogue devel oped by Bevans and Schroeder. Although written nearly ten years earlier, Suess' work expands and further develops it, in my view. Because he writes from within the context of Latin America, Suess supplements the work of Bevans and Schroeder, and gives an emphasis lacking in their work. Suess describes much more concretely what working for justice and peace might look like, and provides guidance for inculturation and dialogue focused on respect, mutuality, and solidarity with the communities receiving missionaries.

TOWARD A METAPHOR OF ACCOMPANIMENT

Some theologians from the United States and Europe have taken seri ously the critique from the former colonies and have proposed a different metaphor for mission, one that takes into account the entire evolution of thinking about the practice of mission work that I have attempted to trace here. For example, based on input from churches in Latin America, the Evangelical Lutheran Church in America (ELCA) now uses the metaphor of *accompaniment* to describe its mission work.

The ELCA defines accompaniment as "walking together in a soli darity that practices interdependence and mutuality. The basis for this *accompaniment*, or what the New Testament calls *koinonia*, is found in the God-human relationship in which God accompanies us in Jesus Christ through the Holy Spirit."[90] Thus, the practice of accompaniment is grounded in a Trinitarian theology based on relationship. However, the Trinitarian theology described in ELCA's vision also integrates procla-ma tion of the Reign of God, as well as the promise of eternal life through Je sus, and thus incorporates the three strains of mission theology articulated in Bevans and Schroeder.[91]

---

89. Ibid., 205.

90. ELCA, *Global Mission in the 21st Century*, 5.

91. Ibid., 7–8.

The ELCA envisions two or more churches walking together in "companionship," with programs and resources blossoming from that companionship—not the other way around. Accompaniment means companionship, and is therefore related to the *fellowship* metaphor proposed by Suess. Companionship involves a conversation between two equals, each of which has gifts to give and to receive, rather than a conversation between giver and receiver.[92]

The ELCA's actual practice of accompaniment is not strikingly different from the practice of prophetic dialogue. The main differences are: ELCA accompaniment takes seriously the critique of theologians such as Suess and Gutierrez, and very firmly respects the agency of local churches; it affirms the need for ecumenical action as constitutive of reconciliation; and it explicitly calls for church-planting. The ELCA describes the practice of mission as: evangelical (proclamation); discipling (the birthing of communities); contextual (transcending familiar cultural forms); holistic (to make incarnate the Reign of God); transforming (prophetic); dialogical (mutual conversations with people of other faiths); ecumenical (seeks to overcome differences among Christians and act with unity); inclusive (embraces the diversity of all peoples); local and global (embraces mission in local as well as global contexts); cruciformed (rejects religious and political domination).[93]

In a later document, which expands further the image of accompaniment, the ELCA describes the heart of mission as reconciliation, which for the church means restoring community with others.[94] This emphasis seems to directly respond to the critique of Suess, that missionaries created an "other" who was an object of mission. Instead, accompaniment incorporates the cultural and historical narratives of all peoples into God's story.[95] God's story is one story, which includes the experiences of all peoples. Finally, the later document appears to move away from the establishment of new communities and toward an "accompaniment" of communities that already exist.[96]

The metaphor of *accompaniment* is widely used by churches in Latin America and the Caribbean. In May 2007 the Conference of Bishops of Latin America and the Caribbean released *Documento de Aparecida*,

92. Ibid., 6.

93. Ibid., 9–11.

94 ELCA, *Accompaniment: A Lens and Methodology for Mission Today*, 5.

95. Ibid., 7.

96. Ibid., 8.

which was the culmination of the work of the 5th General Conference of the Bishops of Latin America and the Caribbean, held in Aparecida, Brazil. Written largely by the current Pope Francis, the document calls for the transformation of the Catholic Church of Latin America and the Ca ribbean into a missionary church.[97] By missionary church, the document means that the church serves in mission to its own people. Although the bulk of the document is devoted to the need for better formation of clergy and lay workers, the word *accompaniment* is used at least thirty times, most often to describe the work of the mission church and of its ministers.

For example, ministers are to accompany migrants and itinerants; the most vulnerable and excluded, so that they may become agents of transformation;[99] victims of violence, displaced people, the disap peared, drug addicts, prostitutes, people with AIDS, abused women and children;[100] families, as well as pregnant girls, single mothers, and broken homes;[101] women, in order to overcome exclusion.[102] The word *accompa niment* is also used multiple times to describe the ministry of formation. In short, although the document never defines the word, *accompaniment* is used as a metaphor for ministry. What this means, it seems to me, is that if outside missionaries use the word *accompaniment* to describe what they do, their work becomes intelligible to the churches of Latin America and the Caribbean.

The *Aparecida* document also contains a very detailed and expanded description of the meaning of "preferential option for the poor," as well as specific indicators of how one's life should witness to the fullness of life in Christ.

> The new life of Jesus Christ touches the entire human being and develops human existence in fullness in its personal, fam- ily, social, and cultural dimensions. That requires entering into a process of change that transfigures the varied aspects of life itself. Only thus will it become possible to recognize that Jesus Christ is our savior in all senses of the word.[104]

97. CELAM, *Documento de Aparecida*, 1.

98. Ibid., 100e; 411.

99. Ibid., 394.

100. Ibid., 402.

101. Ibid., 437.

102. Ibid., 457–58.

103. Ibid., 282, 306, etc.

104. Ibid., 356.

Echoing *Evangelii Nuntiandi*, the document is saying that the primary mode of evangelization is witness through one's own transfigured life to the transforming power of Christ.

"Hedonism" and excessive consumerism obscure the meaning of life and degrade it. So do poverty and inhuman living conditions. Thus, life in Christ involves a movement toward "integral liberation, humanization, reconciliation, and involvement in society."[105] Witnessing to this life in Christ will involve "close affection, listening, humility, solidarity, compassion, dialogue, reconciliation, commitment to social justice, and ability to share."[106]

The preferential option for the poor, which is to be pursued with renewed vigor,[107] is a practice of solidarity, "manifested in visible options and gestures, primarily in defense of life and of the rights of the most vulnerable and excluded, and in continual accompaniment in their efforts to be agents for changing and transforming their situation."[108] It should include aid to meet urgent needs, but is primarily involved with developing more just and equal social and political structures, nationally and internationally.[109] For this reason, the preferential option for the poor "demands that we devote special attention to those Catholic professional people who are responsible for the finances of nations, those who promote employment, and politicians who must create conditions for the economic development of countries, so as to give them ethical guidelines consistent with their faith."[110] Part of this task is to develop actions to influence governments to "enact social and economic policies to deal with the varied needs of the population and lead toward sustainable development."[111] In short, the *Aparecida* document understands mission to include a preferential option for the poor that goes far beyond charitable aid to include:

- Defending the life and the rights of the poor and vulnerable;

- Accompanying the poor in their efforts to be agents of change in their own lives;

105. Ibid., 357–59.
106. Ibid., 363.
107. Ibid., 369.
108. Ibid., 394.
109. Ibid., 384.
110. Ibid., 395.
111. Ibid., 403.

- Influencing the powerful so that they operate in a manner consistent with Catholic teaching; and

- Influencing governments and politicians to change the structures that cause poverty and violence in the first place.

Hector Fabio Henao Gaviria, SJ, Director of the Colombian Conference of Catholic Bishops' National Social Ministry Secretariat since 1996, sheds further light on the meaning of accompaniment for the Latin American churches, especially in a zone of violent conflict. He writes:

> The idea of accompaniment has been one of placing oneself in the situation of those who have directly suffered the atrocities and who, amid so much suffering, have established their autonomy and created alternatives for themselves and their children. Accompaniment demands an active presence that listens and helps communities explore possibilities in greater depth . . . Accompaniment has also involved the collective establishment of dialogue, taking advantage of pastoral space to pray and remember the people who have been disappeared or killed . . . Reconciliation requires a new kind of communication made possible by community accompaniment.[112]

Based on the experience of the Colombian Catholic Church, Fr. Henao Gaviria understands accompaniment as walking together in mutuality and solidarity, but also as more than that. He sees it as an active presence that helps communities to move beyond their suffering, includes prayer and remembrance, and is a prerequisite to reconciliation.

CONCLUSION:
A RECONSTRUCTED MISSION PARADIGM

The reconstructed mission paradigm proposed here accepts mission as *prophetic dialogue* developed by Bevans and Schroeder as a foundation, and expands and further develops their work based on the contributions of mission theology proposed in the global South. I suggest that we use the metaphor of *accompaniment* to describe this paradigm, not because there is anything wrong with prophetic dialogue, but because accompaniment better captures the spirit of mission work that truly transcends the colonial past and respects the agency of local churches and peoples. This paradigm continues the practice of Bevans and Schroeder to take seriously

---

112. Henao Gaviria, "Colombian Church and Peacebuilding," 185.

all three strains of mission theology developed in the twentieth century: mission as founded on the relational Trinity, mission as announcing and enacting the Reign of God, and mission as affirming the uniqueness of Jesus Christ for salvation. However, this paradigm assumes that salvation is not to be found in recruiting for church membership, or in planting new churches. Rather, salvation is to be found in working to usher in the Reign of God, a world where all of God's creation can live in the fulfillment of life. The theology and praxis of mission thus makes a complete break with the colonial and supremacist past of the Christian mission project. However, as we will see, there are significant areas of continuity.

Borrowing from the ELCA, as well as from the Colombian Catholic Church, I define accompaniment as walking together in solidarity, interdependence and mutuality. Accompaniment assumes an active presence among those who suffer, especially those who suffer from poverty and violence, and this presence includes listening and working with communities to overcome their situation. It presumes fellowship and companionship, and as such is based on a foundation of love. It assumes that the missionary is not imposing on the receiving community, but rather that the receiving community has invited his or her presence.

Accompaniment is based in a Trinitarian theology of love, presence, and dialogue. It promotes the universal salvation of Christ through the humble living of Christian values amidst poverty and violence, and by inviting communities to relate their own stories to the Christian narrative. It works toward ushering in the Reign of God through its activities of justice, peace building, community development, and reconciliation.

Maintaining the outline (and most of the components) developed by Bevans and Schroeder, the missionary will engage in the following kinds of activities:

Witness and Proclamation. Today's missionary witnesses to the love of the Trinitarian God, and proclaims the Reign of God and Jesus' saving power primarily through *presence*, through a *humble offering of self to others*, and by *living in accordance with Christian values*. The missionary accepts the suffering of the community she is in, and remains with them, even under dangerous or adverse conditions. The missionary offers his life-giving faith as a gift and in humility, and by his example demonstrates the saving power of Christ.

Liturgy, Prayer, and Contemplation. As described earlier, liturgy and public prayer are the places where overt proclamation of the Gospel takes place. Public prayer should include ecumenical prayer that will witness to Christian unity. Local salvation history, meaning the community's own story, should be included in the liturgical celebration. Further, the contem plative processes of listening and relationship building are foundational to a paradigm of which companionship and solidarity are key components.

Justice, Peace, and Integrity of Creation. The missionary works for jus tice, peace, and integrity of creation by supporting the projects developed by the community itself, and by working at capacity building, such as for mation and organizing, in those communities that require it. The mission ary aims to support the agency of local people to act on their own behalf. The poor, vulnerable, and marginalized speak for themselves to the world's powers, or direct the missionary to challenge the economic and political structures that create poverty, violence and environmental degradation, and to take actions to change national and international policies.

Inculturation. Inculturation is much more than cloaking Christianity in local symbols so that it will be received more easily. Inculturation begins with the story of the community itself, affirms that story as part of God's story, and relates that story to the Christian narrative. In this way the local identity and culture are reinforced, and at the same time the Christian message lives within them.

The Ministry of Reconciliation. Reconciliation is a cornerstone of mis sion. Ecumenical and interreligious dialogue and action are part of a min istry of reconciliation, and can include the creation of ecumenical and/or interfaith communities acting together. A ministry of reconciliation in volves reaching out to all sides involved in conflict or disunity, recognizing the image of Christ in each person. It also involves liturgical celebrations of healing and unity.

Dialogue. Dialogue, or conversation, is foundational to all of the elements of missionary activity, and begins with presence and companionship. A relationship founded on love and companionship begins with respectful conversation. Listening to the story of a community involves being part of a conversation. Ecumenical and interreligious dialogue is a mutual ex change that starts as a conversation. Supporting the justice, peace, and development projects of the community involves a conversation about the nature of those projects and how one can be of service to them.

Each of these elements of mission will be discussed more thoroughly in the next chapter.

Although a reconstructed mission paradigm makes a break with the colonial past, there are significant areas of overlap with all of the theologies and practices reviewed in this chapter. In particular, I noted at the outset that any contemporary missiology must relate to the New Testament approaches to mission. A brief comparison of the elements of a new paradigm elaborated above, with the elements of mission in the New Testament described at the beginning of this chapter confirms a great deal of continuity. Like the New Testament practice of mission, a paradigm of accompaniment:

- Is political, even revolutionary, because it challenges the structures that create poverty, violence, and division.

- Creates new relationships that cross the boundaries of culture, religion, and socioeconomic status.

- Stays with the mission, suffering with the people, even up to martyrdom.

- Witnesses to the Reign of God by practicing justice and love.

- Works for economic justice, peace, and reconciliation.

- Involves a fellowship of believers bound together by prayer.

- Views Christian unity as part of the ushering in of the Reign of God.

- Is not undertaken for the sake of the church, but for the sake of the world.

In this section I have taken the elements of missionary activity developed by Bevans and Schroder as a response to the excesses of the colonial period, and developed and refined them so that they more clearly and overtly point to a relationship based in love, solidarity, and mutuality, and so that they respect the capacity of all people to be agents of their own and their community's transformation. In the next chapter I will examine the praxis of international protective accompaniment, to see how it is a model, or example, of this revised mission paradigm.

4

International Accompaniment as Christian Mission

A Theology and Praxis of Christian Mission in Zones of Violent Conflict

THE PREVIOUS CHAPTER PROPOSED using the metaphor "accompaniment" to describe a theology of Christian mission that is appropriate for the changing world of the twenty-first century. Accompaniment is defined as walking together in solidarity, interdependence, and mutuality. "Walking together" implies an active presence among those who suffer from poverty and violence, and this active presence listens to, and works with, communities to overcome their situation. An accompaniment mission is based in presence, companionship, and fellowship. It occurs as a result of an invitation from the host, or receiving, communities. It involves witnessing to Christian faith, but not imposing it. And it strives to transform situations of poverty and violence. The components of accompaniment are: witness and proclamation; liturgy, prayer, and contemplation; working for justice, peace, and integrity of creation; inculturation; the ministry of reconciliation; and dialogue.

This chapter more fully develops the elements of a theology of accompaniment described in chapter 3 and brings them together with the elements of international protective accompaniment described by the accompanied communities in chapter 2, making the case that this theology of accompaniment correlates significantly with what leaders of accompanied communities say about international protective accompaniment. This chapter offers additional examples of accompaniment, beyond those given in chapter 2, including some from my own experience. This chapter thus elaborates a theology and praxis of Christian mission in a zone of violent conflict.

The following sections discuss each of the six elements of an accompaniment mission in greater detail, and, using the work of CPT as an example, illustrate the ways in which international protective accompaniment can be viewed as a praxis within the accompaniment metaphor. I also believe that there are major lessons here for mission in all contexts, not just conflict zones. The elements of mission appropriate for a zone of violent conflict can also be translated for use in other places and contexts.

I am using the work of CPT as an example, and as a result, the illustrations provided here present CPT in the best possible light. Obviously, the practice on the ground varies and is often dependent on the composition of teams at any given time. This chapter shows CPT as its best self, and also calls on the other mission groups to incorporate CPT's best work in zones of violent conflict.

WITNESS AND PROCLAMATION

A missionary witnesses to the saving power of the Cross, and to the values inherent in the concept of the Reign of God. Through the example of her life, the missionary demonstrates the saving power of Christ. Witness is the essential and primary form of evangelization, and is itself proclamation of the Good News. Missionaries must first and foremost *become* the values they proclaim.

From its inception, the purpose of CPT has been to witness to the biblical concepts of justice, peace, and reconciliation. "The goal of CPT would be to witness to Jesus Christ as we seek to identify with the suffering, promote peace, reduce violence, identify with those caught in violence and oppression and foster justice by using the techniques of nonviolent direct action."[1] The theological underpinnings of the organization are based on proclamation of Jesus through a biblically based peace witness.[2] A peace witness includes presenting a nonviolent alternative to war, and has its biblical foundations in the Sermon on the Mount, and in the respect for human life elaborated in the first chapter of Genesis. Witnessing is not aimed at converting people in at-risk communities to Christianity. Rather, it is aimed at living out a biblically based commitment to justice

1. Kern, *In Harm's Way*, 5.
2. Ibid., 9.

and peace within those communities, and thereby proclaiming the saving power of Christ.

CPT's work is to be present with suffering communities, and the leaders I interviewed named this as the most important aspect of CPT's accompaniment:

> Through their presence among the communities . . . this way of being a witness gives us much courage, and gives us the certainty that we are not alone in this process and in this fight.[3]

CPT teams live simply and communally, not above the standard of living of the communities where they work. And CPT projects regularly denounce economic injustice and violence, taking prophetic stands, especially against the policies of the United States and Canada—primarily through articles published regularly on their website and listserve and in their newsletter, but also through occasional lobbying, and reporting and advocating with embassy personnel. In chapter 2, we saw that this aspect of witness, the reporting aspect, was identified as a key role of accompaniment.

A particular charism of CPT accompaniment is witnessing to the Cross through suffering with communities hard-hit by violence, even to the point of taking on that suffering personally. I experienced it myself when, in September 2004, along with a colleague, I was attacked and brutally beaten by Israeli settlers working out of an illegal outpost in Palestinian territory on the West Bank. We were walking Palestinian children to school past an Israeli settlement where residents had brutalized Palestinians in the past. CPT's hope was that the presence of international volunteers would dissuade further violence. Instead, on that morning the violence was turned against us, the accompaniers. I suffered a fractured elbow and a knee injury that has left me in frequent pain, and my colleague suffered a punctured lung. We both had cuts and bruises to our faces and hands. The children were frightened but unharmed; the accompaniers were the target of the violence, not the accompanied.

This attack took place just two days after CPT had officially opened a project in the South Hebron Hills area of Palestinian territory. Before CPT was present, Palestinians had suffered regular violence at the hands of the settlers, with little recourse, because reporting incidents to the Israeli police and military—the entities in charge of security in Palestinian territory—brought little response. Palestinians felt they could either endure

---

3. Ubencel Duque, interview with author.

the violence in silence, or take up arms. Once CPT established itself in the area, Palestinians were given a nonviolent option: the option to denounce the violence and harassment publicly to the international community and press. CPT's presence and denouncement of the violence has afforded the community a certain amount of protection; to this day they have neither taken up arms nor displaced, and, despite continued violence and threats of violence by nearby Israeli settlers, CPT remains with the community.

There are numerous other examples of members of CPT taking on the risk of violence in an attempt to protect the communities they accompany. In Colombia, some of that risk has involved attempting to dialogue with armed actors. In Micoahumado, those dialogues took place under the auspices of an organized community process; however, members of CPT can also find themselves faced with the possibility of spontaneous dialogue, as described below:

> Just before the sun set on Saturday, November 24 (2001), a group of about sixteen armed men in civilian clothes waved CPTers William Payne and Matt Schaaf, along with their boat driver, to the riverbank. Payne disembarked to hand out literature to the group and explained that CPTers do not believe in any weapons, including these particular guns, and that CPT is not connected to any armed group.
>
> Apparently growing tired of their message of nonviolence, the leader of the group, a heavyset man with a large silver revolver, told Payne and Schaaf they could continue on upriver. They did, and after dropping off the motorist in a safer area, the CPTers turned the boat around to continue the dialogue with the armed men, believed by the local community to be right-wing paramilitaries.[4]

This incident took place while CPT was accompanying communities along the Opon River at a time when the area was part of a land dispute between guerrilla, paramilitary, and Colombian state forces. In this example, CPT's witness was directed toward armed paramilitaries. In other cases, taking on risk simply involves being present when armed actors are threatening a community or family.

> Two CPTers heard an eight-year-old girl running toward them scream, "They're going to kill my Daddy!" as nine paramilitary members with machine guns entered her family's yard on

4. Christian Peacemaker Teams, "Colombia: Paramilitaries Create Fear in Opon River Region," http://www.cpt.org/cptnet/2001/11/30/colombia-paramilitaries-create-fear-op-n-river-region.

Tuesday, June 15, 2004. The CPTers arrived to see members of the illegal right-wing armed group United Self Defense Forces, Central Bolivar Bloc (AUC-BCB) insulting and threatening to kill the girl's father in front of his family, children, and friends. A guerrilla fighter from the Revolutionary Armed Forces of Colombia—People's Army (FARC-EP), whom the paramilitaries had captured a few hours earlier, accused the girl's father of collaborating with that left-wing armed group.

Within minutes of CPT arriving at the property, the paramilitaries left the terrorized family and continued their march downriver. CPTers stayed with the family, praying to God for protection and peace. Everyone present said that if CPT had not been present, the paramilitaries would have killed the man.[5]

In both of the above examples, CPT's willingness to take on risk in order to protect the communities they are accompanying also involves presenting an alternative to taking up arms when facing armed actors. CPT is witnessing to the power of Cross—to non-violent self-sacrifice for the sake of a greater good—and particularly to the Cross being more powerful than the sword.

CPT's witness is not only focused on armed groups, or on the at-risk communities where the accompaniment takes place. CPT's mandate is also to witness, to the North American and European Christian Churches, the biblically based call to work for justice and peace. The original call to create CPT was directed toward churches, congregations, and church agencies, and was at least partly a call to reform them from within.[6] outreach work is directed toward those entities, in an effort to gain much broader support from within Christianity for the mission of witnessing to justice and peace. In this way, Christians are encouraged and enabled to answer the call to work for justice and peace, and this, as we saw in chapter 1, addresses structural causes of the world's violence and injustice.

We have already seen that this form of witness, meaning witnessing to the biblical call to justice and peace to communities that already call themselves Christian, is a crucial aspect of the missionary vocation in today's world, where Christianity has taken hold globally, but seeks to coexist with other faith traditions. Christians are not called so much to convert others as to become better Christians ourselves. This involves presence, companionship, solidarity, and sharing one's life with the

5. Christian Peacemaker Teams, "They Are Going to Kill My Daddy," http://www.cpt.org/cptnet/2004/06/20/colombia-ampquottheyo39re-going-kill-my-daddyampquot.

6. Christian Peacemaker Teams, "History," http://www.cpt.org/about/history.

receiving community. The missionary lives simply and humbly offers her faith to the community. This offering of oneself means living the Christian values of justice, peace, and integrity of creation, and working alongside the community to usher them in. This includes taking prophetic stands against economic injustice or violence. It also means suffering with the community and staying with them, even when the missionary herself is in danger. In becoming better Christians, others may be drawn to our faith, or they may seek a similar renewal within their own faith traditions. Either way, the world would evolve closer to the vision of God articulated in the Old and New Testaments.

Witness and proclamation are connected to the other aspects of an accompaniment mission, because the other elements elaborate the details of the Good News that accompaniers are proclaiming in a zone of violent conflict. To begin with, inculturation helps the missionary to understand the appropriate ways to transmit a Christian witness in a particular context.

INCULTURATION

Inculturation involves identifying the core values underlying the Christian faith and finding convergence between them and the core values of a given culture. True inculturation discovers ways to embody faith that make sense in a given cultural context. By culture, I am referring to three elements: values, ethos (the actuality of a population's existence, with its deprivations, hopes, fears, successes, and failures), and worldview (their idea of the way the world should be).[7] Inculturation means the Gospel and its values will be visible in people's lives and in their culture. Inculturation begins with the story of the community itself, affirms that story as part of God's story, and relates that story to the Christian narrative. In this way the local identity and culture are reinforced, and at the same time the Christian message lives within them. In addition, Gospel values can be counter-cultural, and inculturation in a given context may also involve challenging the dominant culture. In this section I discuss the first aspect of inculturation, that which correlates the community's story with the Gospel story. In subsequent sections I elaborate Gospel values that are counter-cultural but also life-giving in a conflict zone.

Put very simply, violence shatters a person's or a people's identity and their worldview, and this in turn affects the local culture. If the Gospel is to make sense to a local culture, a certain kind of inculturation is required

7. Gittins, "Beyond Liturgical Inculturation," 48–50.

in contexts that have been affected by violence. Inculturation in contexts of violent conflict involves connecting the story of communities that have suffered from oppression, violence, or displacement, with the story of Jesus suffering on the Cross. This is a connection that Padre Raphael in Tiquisio has made very clearly by placing the names of the community's dead and disappeared above the altar, together with the crucifix. This kind of preaching of the Gospel is a true inculturation: the community is relat ing its own story to the story of Jesus. The identity of the community thus becomes connected to the Gospel narrative.

The altar at Iglesia Santismo Cristo in Tiquisio. The sheets of paper hanging on either side of the crucifix list the names of dead and disappeared. The banners to the far right and far left are the names of community leaders murdered. The murder of their leaders is what galvanized the community to organize.

Making this connection assumes a spirituality of mission based on the saving power of the Cross. CPT, and especially individual members of CPT, frequently connects its work to the Cross in its publications and public actions. One example of this was an activity I participated in at the fence that has been constructed along the border between the United

States and Mexico. During the spring and summer of 2005, the CPT team that was staffing a project in Arizona began painting crosses on the border fence to commemorate those who died attempting to migrate from Mexico to the United States.

The author paints crosses on the US-Mexico border wall
outside of Douglas, Arizona.

This activity was meant to make the connection between migrant deaths and the suffering of Jesus on the Cross. The witness was aimed at the Border Patrol and vigilante groups active in that area of the border, as well as at groups of migrants crossing in that area. We were comparing migrants who had died in the desert to the suffering of Jesus on the Cross. As a result, we had a number of interesting conversations with Border Patrol agents who encountered our work, which gave us the opportunity to witness to the life and dignity of the migrants whom they encounter each day.

Jim Loney, a former member of CPT's leadership, was kidnapped along with two colleagues by Iraqi insurgents while leading a CPT delegation in Iraq in late 2005. After his liberation by British Special Forces, Loney wrote this reflection:

> Christ teaches us to love our enemies, do good to those who harm us, pray for those who persecute us. He calls us to accept suffering before we inflict injury. He calls us to pick up the cross and to lay down the sword. We will most certainly fail in this call. I did. And I'll fail again. This does not change Christ's teaching that violence itself is the tomb, violence is the dead-end. Peace won through the barrel of a gun might be a victory but it is not peace. Our captors had guns and they ruled over us. Our rescuers had bigger guns and ruled over the captors. We were freed, but the rule of the gun stayed. The stone across the tomb of violence has not been rolled away.[8]

In this reflection, Loney experiences violence as the tomb, and the Cross as liberation. Anyone who has experienced violent conflict will recognize violence as the tomb. But understanding the Cross as liberation is more complicated, because Christianity contains dueling theologies of the Cross: one more liberating, and the other that can promote passivity, with the latter being far more common. Whichever theology of the Cross the missionary promotes can either lead to a life-giving inculturation, or to one that leaves a community affected by violence grappling with its faith and feeling abandoned by God. I make this point because a lack of theological reflection on this issue can do more harm than good in a conflict zone, and missionaries working in these regions should receive very careful formation.

Some examples will illustrate the point. Ricardo Falla, SJ, anthropologist and Jesuit priest, conducted a study of violence and torture during the civil war in Guatemala. Falla tells the story of a torture victim who was seized and transported by helicopter to a military base in Playa Grande, a regional center. His captors put him in a kind of tunnel where he could sit up, but not stand or lie down. They tortured him through simulated

8. Loney, "*From the Tomb*," para. 18–19.

drowning and asphyxiation, trying to get him to admit he was a guerrilla. But he was not a guerrilla, and he never changed his story. Instead of breaking down, the victim prayed constantly, and was able to identify with the crucified Christ who was himself tortured and put to death, and with God who feels his pain. Through identifying his pain with the experience of Christ, the victim was able to feel "a ray of consolation and hope, that there was life."[9] The love and consolation he felt through identification with Christ converged with the love he felt for his family and his co-workers in the field, and as a result he was not broken by the experience.

Many other torture victims in Guatemala succumbed to the military's strategy of violence and domination. As a result of his research, however, Falla believes that the strategy can be resisted through identification with Christ in the midst of torture.[10] Identification with Christ in the midst of torture presupposes that the victim's religious identity was already aligned with the crucified Christ, and that she could then rely on that identity during moments of extreme vulnerability.

The experience of connecting one's suffering to the crucified Christ as being life-giving in the midst of torture is not limited to this single story. Fr. Michael Lapsley, a priest from New Zealand, was expelled from South Africa in 1976 for his work in support of undoing apartheid. On April 28, 1990, a period in which the South African government was under enormous pressure to negotiate the end of apartheid, Fr. Lapsley received a letter bomb at his home in Zimbabwe. The bomb blew off both his hands. Fr. Lapsley reveals:

> I felt the presence of God with me in that bombing, sharing in my crucifixion. In the midst of indescribable pain, I also felt that Mary the mother of Jesus who had watched her son being crucified somehow understood what it was I was going through.[11]

Fr. Lapsley experienced God as accompanying him in his suffering, and as a result was able to turn his suffering into something that was life-giving for others: he later became chaplain of a trauma center for victims of violence in Cape Town.

Unfortunately, this life-giving image of God and Christ crucified is not the only, or even the most common, approach to the Cross. Another example illustrates this point. Between 1915 and 1922 the Armenian

---

9 Falla, *Mascares de la Selva*: 33.

10. Ibid.

11. Lapsley, "Bearing the Pain in Our Bodies," 20.

population in Turkey was reduced from two million to several hundred thousand. Between one million and one and a half million Armenians lost their lives in forced marches and massacres. Armenia, the location of some of the most ancient Christian sites and relics, lost many of the oldest centers of Christian culture, as well as its historic monuments. One Armenian writer describes the effects on Armenians today:

> Anger at God, sometimes leading to a complete denial of God, is a well-known phenomenon among survivors of the Armeno-cide and their children. "How could God have allowed this to happen, especially to a people who were the first to adopt Christianity as a state religion?" And there is the always present voice which raises the disturbing rumination, "Armenians wonder if God is on their side."[12]

Vigen Guroian, an Armenian who studies survivors, goes on to say that as a result of their history, Armenian identity is tied strongly with Christianity, and at the same time Armenians feel angry toward God for allowing the genocide to happen. This combination has led to "an impossible mix of hatred of God and of self-hatred."[13] This stems from a worldview that sees God as in total control of the universe, and as allowing unjust suffering to happen. In this approach, to be like Jesus, Christians must passively accept suffering as God's will, and extreme suffering is meted out as a kind of punishment for misbehaving.

We have seen two very different interpretations of Christ crucified, stemming from two very different images of God, and leading to two very different ways of dealing with violence. In one interpretation, Christ crucified is not suffering for the sake of suffering, but rather suffering for the sake of a larger vision. Christ did not seek the crucifixion, and suffering is not something God wants people to seek. When unjust suffering happens, the victim can recognize herself in Christ crucified, certain that God is with her. In recognizing this, she understands that God is accompanying her, and this gives her the strength to continue. In the other interpretation, Christ crucified means accepting violence because that was the sacrifice of Jesus on the cross, and that is what God asks. It seems to me that this is the version that can also lead to other kinds of passive acceptance of violence, such as victims of domestic violence staying with their spouses. This version, which sees God as all-powerful and all-controlling, also seems to

12. Guroian, "When Remembering Brings Redemption," 78.
13. Ibid.

lead people to believe that God has abandoned them in their suffering, or that suffering is a form of punishment.

In short, an appropriate inculturation of the Gospel in a zone of violent conflict involves finding ways to connect suffering with the experience of Christ crucified. However, the way that this is communicated matters greatly, and thus the theological and spiritual formation of missionaries is crucial. Believing that an all-powerful God has caused the suffering is very different than believing that God is accompanying us in our suffering. The image of God as accompanying us also provides the foundation for our accompaniment metaphor for mission. Further, we can connect the idea that God is accompanying us to the Incarnation: through the presence of Jesus, God communicated to us that God is with us. In the same way, missionaries accompany the suffering, communicating to them that God is with them.

It is important to insert a caveat here. In Colombia, the majority of the population is Christian and so most Colombians already connect their identity to Christianity in some way. A mission of international protective accompaniment in a non-Christian context would not attempt to connect the identities of the population to Christ crucified. This would amount to trying to sever the peoples' connection to the religion of their ancestors, and could shatter identities already made fragile by violence, and ultimately make things worse. In this context, the missionary:

- Lives her faith and values and humbly shares them with others, never imposing anything, but showing the transformational power of Christianity through the example of her life.

- Through the presence of accompaniment, communicates his understanding that God is accompanying the community in its suffering.

We have seen that inculturation in a conflict zone involves identifying one's suffering with the suffering Christ. But it also involves much more. The Gospel message does not end with the Cross. Our faith is life-giving because after the Cross we find resurrection. The missionary must also become part of the people's struggle for life, so that they are brought down from the Cross. Resurrection in a conflict zone involves addressing the root causes of the violence, and also transformation of the conflict itself, ultimately leading to reconciliation. These are the topics addressed in the next two elements of accompaniment, and which introduce an inculturation of the Gospel that may be counter-cultural in a conflict zone.

WORKING FOR JUSTICE, PEACE, AND INTEGRITY OF CREATION

In an accompaniment model, the missionary supports projects developed by the community itself, and works at capacity-building, such as training, formation, leadership development and organizing, in those communities that request it. Capacity-building supports and assists local people to act on their own behalf to address the root causes of their suffering. In this way an accompaniment mission addresses the reasons why a community is on the Cross in the first place.

This work is founded on a biblically based spirituality of nonviolence. In the Beatitudes, we are told that the peacemaker is blessed. The Sermon on the Mount continues with suggestions for nonviolent ways to resolve our conflicts. But nonviolence has its foundation primarily in the first chapter of Genesis, where we are reminded that all people are created in the image and likeness of God. Respect for the life of each human person calls us to put an end to the violations of human dignity—such as extreme poverty, displacement, human rights abuses, and murder—found in zones of violent conflict. Respect for the dignity of life, as well as a preference for seeking nonviolent solutions to conflict, are Christian values frequently found lacking in a zone of violent conflict, and is what is meant here by a counter-cultural inculturation.

This aspect of CPT's work was discussed at length in chapter 2, where we saw that a reduction in violence was one of the key effects of inter national protective accompaniment. We also saw that the communities perceive that denouncing the injustice and the violence internationally, and creating the space to do so domestically, is a primary role that interna tional accompaniers play. And we saw that international accompaniment helped to create the space necessary to prevent communities from displac ing, thereby enabling them to organize and develop sustainable economic projects for their communities. We also saw that international protective accompaniment takes place only at the invitation of the communities and is directed by them. Finally, we saw that some of the key spiritual lead ers of the communities I interviewed spoke about the importance of the Christian values of nonviolence and respect for human life in the midst of violent conflict.

Based on these results, it seems fair to state that it is possible and even probable that if hundreds or even thousands of teams were placed in at-risk communities located in conflict zones around the globe, they could play a role in transforming those conflicts.

The study in chapter 2 also provided an assessment of the work of CPT in particular, and thus some guidelines for other organizations interested in becoming involved in international protective accompaniment work. The communities emphasized presence as the most important aspect of accompaniment, and, as we have seen, CPT does that very well. But the communities also viewed denouncing the violence, injustice, and human rights abuses to the foreign powers that in many ways control their destiny as an important way to address the structural causes of their problems. They also felt that formation, capacity building, and financial support for economic development projects is the way that communities will sustain themselves in the long run, which in turn prevents future violence from breaking out. CPT's work, and in this way they are similar to other mission groups, has historically not been as strong in these areas.

With respect to advocacy work, individual members of CPT from time to time engage in advocacy work by visiting US government officials, such as members of Congress or embassy personnel. In addition, CPT teams occasionally send out "action alerts" to their email listserve comprised of individuals, organizations, and congregations, asking them to write letters to the US Congress or to some other government entity. Unfortunately, these campaigns are not supported organizationally with staff specifically devoted to advocacy, or with a developed, coherent plan or strategy. It is fair to say that working to affect churches will in turn affect voters, at least in the United States, and so that is a form of advocacy work. But it is not the only form of advocacy work that communities in conflict zones are requesting. Without requiring an enormous increase in resources, CPT could work more closely with the multitude of other advocacy organizations to put forward the agenda of the communities it serves. CPT's hands-on experience in the middle of conflict zones is a voice that should be heard in policy discussions.

With respect to economic development, we have seen that poverty is a major fuel of conflict, because many young people join armed groups out of poverty, and because the roots of conflict involve control over land and resources. If we want peace, we need to work for economic justice, as Pope Paul VI told us. While this is not the expertise of Christian Peacemaker Teams, it might be possible to CPT to use its own network of churches and organizations to connect communities with sponsors who could assist them.

These suggestions for improving the work of CPT came from the leadership of communities that CPT accompanies, and are guidelines for any effective accompaniment mission in a zone of violent conflict. A comprehensive accompaniment project includes networking widely with other organizations and resources, so that presence on the ground can translate into addressing the structural causes of the violence. In addition, a mission of justice and peace must look at transformation of the conflict so that warring factions cease to view each other as the enemy. This is a ministry of reconciliation, the next element.

THE MINISTRY OF RECONCILIATION

Reconciliation lies at the heart of this entire investigation and book. Chapter 2 pointed out that the roots of the present conflict in Colombia lie in the colonial period, when specific groups of people—especially in digenous and those of African ancestry—were forced to the periphery of the country. Chapter 3 looked at the history of Christian mission and the damage that was done, again especially to indigenous and people of Afri can ancestry. In constructing a new paradigm for mission, I am seeking to discover whether there is a way to undo, or at least mitigate, the injustices that the Christian mission project is at least partially responsible for, and that also lie at the heart of many present-day conflicts, including the one in Colombia. The practice of reconciliation is where those answers lie.

Reconciliation encompasses forgiveness, but entails more than forgiveness. Christianity asks us to seek reconciliation, but there is little guidance on how to do so, or what it might look like if we found it. After I was attacked and beaten in Palestine, numerous well-meaning friends and acquaintances suggested that I needed to "forgive" my attackers. At the time, forgiveness was the last thing on my mind. I was focused on healing, and on making sense of what had happened. Offering forgiveness to my attackers felt like it would be offering healing to them when I was not yet healed myself, and thus placing their healing before my own. I think that this is a trap that Christian teaching on reconciliation can lead to for the victim: we think we must forgive immediately, and that if we cannot, somehow we risk our relationship with God.

Those exhortations to forgive did have the positive effect of leading me to reflect on the meaning of forgiveness and what it might look like in my case. I did not know the identities of my attackers because they were masked, and they have never been found by the authorities. So in my case I was being asked to forgive unknown assailants who were members of a specific community of Jewish settlers in occupied Palestine. But how? My allegiance was with the Palestinians I was accompanying, who lived on the territory long before the arrival of the current state of Israel, and have been harassed, threatened, beaten, displaced, and demonized. I was accompanying children who were simply trying to get to school.

However, in a previous job, in the 1980s, I worked with an organization dedicated to the rights of Soviet Jews, a discriminated-against minority in the former Soviet Union. Many of the Jewish settlers in Palestine are refugees from what is now Russia and were denied permission to emigrate under Soviet rule but were allowed to depart in the late 1980s and early 1990s. These "refuseniks," as they were called, were marginalized by Soviet society, and many left Russia as soon as they could. Some settled in the United States, but most are in Israel. They are now living alongside people who contributed to the founding of the state of Israel: refugees from Nazi Germany. This is a population well aware of its own history as victims of genocide. My reflecting on what happened to me led me to believe that this history explains the need of the Jewish people to protect their identity as a people and also their desire for their own homeland—as well as their fear of what might happen if they lost it.

Through this reflection, I came to empathize with my attackers. This is not the same as saying I condone what they did. I believe they should be brought to justice, and I also believe that their history does not, and never can, justify seizing the homeland of another people. However, I empathize, and I believe that empathy is the meaning of forgiveness in my case.

Forgiveness is not the same as reconciliation. Reconciliation is much bigger, and would entail the attackers and their community, the Palestinian children and their community, and me and my team of accompaniers coming together to create a new vision for life together, one that embodies the Reign of God, as captured, for example, in Isaiah 11:1–10. In this world, no one would be marginalized or demonized; everyone would have what they need to live in dignity, and people would stop killing each other. We humans are a long way from this.

In order to get there, people embroiled in conflict would need to foster a new identity, one that makes room for the identity of the other in their understanding of their own identity. Miroslav Volf, who writes about reconciliation from his experience in Croatia during the Balkan War, explores what kind of selves, or identities, people need to foster in order to live in harmony with people who are different from us. He suggests that theologians need to concentrate on forming "social agents capable of envisioning and creating just, truthful, and peaceful societies, and on shaping a cultural climate in which such agents will thrive."[14] Speaking of

14. Volf, *Exclusion and Embrace*, 19–21.

Christians, Volf says that if we are serious about pursuing reconciliation, we must be able to adjust our identities to make room for the other, and this is a prerequisite for the embrace, or reconciliation, of the other. As Christians, then, we must remain a part of our own culture with its particularities, while at the same time fully taking on a Christian identity that welcomes differences as internal to its culture.[15] Volf is suggesting that a truly Christian identity, based in reconciliation as a core principle, is one that embraces all people as created in God's image. For Christians, this means that we are one human family and there is no "other." This speaks to the Church taking on a counter-cultural role involving spiritual formation of its members into a Christian culture that embraces differences, including religious differences. Embracing differences means that populations seek out the common good of all, rather than clinging to past hurts and transgressions.

However, the full embrace cannot happen in a conflict zone until the truth has been spoken and justice done. In other words, the process of adjusting our identities to make room for the other, including our enemy, includes speaking the truth about what has happened and rectifying the injustice. Speaking the truth and rectifying the injustice includes an apology and expression of remorse to the victims for wrongs committed. Full reconciliation could not happen in my case, because the injustice has not been rectified. In a larger sense, reconciliation is not possible until the issues that fuel the conflict are resolved, meaning the elimination of the structural inequities that led to the oppression in the first place.

In the case of Colombia, the roots of the conflict go deep, and have to do with poverty, land rights, and the marginalization of certain population groups. True reconciliation would begin with speaking the truth about what has happened to these groups, and addressing their concerns. It would have to take into account the perspective of all sides, because everyone needs to speak their truth. After truth has been spoken and justice done, essential moments in the movement from what Volf calls "exclusion to embrace" are repentance on the part of the oppressor, forgiveness on the part of the victim, healing of memory, and making space in oneself for the identity of the other.[16] This latter point refers to what was stated above: for Christians, taking on a counter-cultural Christian identity that embraces differences as an integral part of one's own identity. These essential moments would be practiced by both sides in a conflict, because often the

15. Ibid., 47–48.
16. Ibid., 29–30; 100.

lines between victim and oppressor are blurred in a conflict zone. Israel/ Palestine is a good example of this. The embrace of reconciliation must be mutual, which means that both sides have become equal partners in the conversation.

South African theologian John De Gruchy, speaking from his experience with healing from apartheid, affirms much of Volf's perspective. He proposes that reconciliation cannot be pursued until the alienated parties are willing to face each other. The first step is meeting and listening to the "other." But this presupposes that the "other" is regarded as an equal conversation partner. The second step is the willingness to listen to the other side of the story, even if one remains unconvinced of its merit. Reconciliation becomes possible when we are able to open ourselves up to the perspective of the other, and, without surrendering our own identities, exchange places with the other in a conversation that "takes us beyond ourselves."[17]

Like Volf, De Gruchy understands truth as a prerequisite to reconciliation. However, truth telling has its limitations, for we can never arrive at or understand the whole truth. No one is impartial; truth tellers always see things from a particular perspective. But truth telling can reclaim a history that has been "denied and shredded," even if every fact is not uncovered. It can provide data for an encounter with the truth that is part of the process of reconciliation.[18] A key part of truth telling must be listening to the rage of victims, for in the telling of their stories they are empowered.[19] This whole process can lead to a conversion among the conversation partners, and therefore a moving toward a new future—toward the embrace, in Volf's terminology.[20]

In my own imaginary scenario this would mean that the three parties involved in the attack (me and my community of accompaniers, the Palestinian children and their community, and the Jewish attackers and their community) would face each other and hear each other speak the truth of their experience. The hope is that this would lead to empathy on all sides, and a movement away from positions that seek only what one perceives as the good for one's personal community, and instead to seek life together and the good of all.

17. De Gruchy, *Reconciliation: Restoring Justice*, 152–53.
18. Ibid., 154–62.
19. Ibid., 169–70.
20. Ibid., 162–64.

Robert Schreiter proposes that the victim must initiate this process of reconciliation, not the oppressor, and that the object of reconciliation is the humanity, or conversion, of the oppressor. In other words, the point is to bring about a change of heart within the oppressor, so that he or she views the victim as equally human, created in God's image. And in reality, it is God who takes the initiative, because it is only through God's grace that the victim is able to forgive.[21] But we can contribute to the work of God's grace through the steps described above, which empower the victim, and enable her to be open to God's grace in her life.

This analysis assumes that there is a clear line between victim and oppressor, but, as noted earlier, this is not always the case in a conflict zone. Often atrocities are committed by all sides. In reality, the object is the humanity of everyone involved, and reaching the fullness of our humanity can only happen through an encounter with the Divine, in whose image we are created.

I would not have been able to initiate a process of reconciliation with my attackers until I had experienced healing myself, and fundamentally healing comes from God. In this sense reconciliation is more a spirituality than a strategy, because it begins with experiencing God's grace in our own lives and leads to a commitment to a reconciling way of life. Reconciliation is more than just forgiveness on the part of the victim and repentance on the part of the oppressor, because true reconciliation leads to a new way of being, which Schreiter calls a "new creation."[22] Schreiter proposes that the Christian churches can play an important role through educating people in this spirituality of reconciliation, in praying for it through rituals, and in creating communities that sustain and nurture reconciliation.[23]

Mennonite theologian and peacebuilder John Paul Lederach hints at what a new, reconciled creation might involve. He stresses that a group's identity is linked to what its members remember and keep alive. A history of oppression by one group against another creates a collective memory that is passed across generations. The deepest history of a group he calls "narrative," and narrative is defined as the formative stories of genesis and place. The formation of group identity arising from the past, its construction of the future, and its survival as a group are connected to finding place, voice, and story; in other words, to its narrative. Conflict can be imaged as narrative broken, meaning that the story of a people is broken

21. Schreiter, *Reconciliation: Mission and Ministry in Changing Social Order*
22. Ibid., 55–63.
23. Schreiter, *Ministry of Reconciliation: Spirituality and Strategies*, 127–30.

or marginalized by a dominant culture, and in this way meaning, identity, and place in history are lost for the marginalized group.

As with most protracted conflicts seen today, the roots of the present-day Colombia conflict lie in the history of European colonization. Colonization decimated indigenous populations, and the survivors in many cases lost their traditional lands and livelihoods. African slaves were taken from their homelands and forced into labor, millions dying in the process. The Christian mission project imposed European religion on indigenous and African people, denying them their ancestral understanding of the Divine. Their identities were stolen. Eventually, out of this situation arose guerrilla groups to fight for the land rights of marginalized populations, and paramilitary groups to protect the land rights of the elite. This is the broken narrative that Lederach talks about.

In a true reconciliation process, there must be public acknowledgement of what happened, who suffered, who was responsible, and how they have been held accountable, in order for the communities affected to begin to find their place, story, and voice again. Once that happens, for reconciliation to occur, there must be a "restorying," a finding of a new narrative together that gives meaning to life and to ongoing relationships between the groups. The art of restorying lies between memory of the past and potential for the future. Restorying does not erase the past or repeat it. It uses the imagination to generate a new future together.[24]

Restorying takes on a very concrete meaning in many conflict zones today, where members of armed groups come from the same towns and villages, and the person who murdered one's family member may live in the village down the road. A reconciliation process seeks to bring population groups to a place where they can live together in peace, without dredging up old fights for centuries into the future.

Full reconciliation always lies in the future. It is connected to the Reign of God, which we strive to bring about in the here and now but which is always beyond us to achieve. Christians believe that we are fully reconciled only in God. Instead, what we are seeking is a "non-final" reconciliation that allows us to live in peace with one another.[25] However, there are specific actions that can be taken and specific stages of reconciliation: it is a process initiated by the victims, and involves forgiveness by the victims and repentance by the perpetrators, requires dialogue, and

24. Lederach, *Moral Imagination*, 142–49.

25 Volf, *Exclusion and Embrace*, 109–10, and De Gruchy, *Reconciliation: Restoring Justice*, 154.

leads to envisioning a new future, which requires restorying together. This process presumes that truth has been told and justice accomplished.

In my view, an accompaniment model of mission is itself part of a reconciliation process, because it addresses the effects of colonialism and seeks to empower communities that have suffered those effects. The sec tions below pull out a number of elements from the above discussion of the nature of reconciliation, and illustrate the ways that a model of ac companiment realizes them.

Presence: Empowering the Victim

The reconciliation process depends on the victim. The victim needs to feel that truth has been told and justice done, and thus must feel ready to initi ate a process of reconciliation with the perpetrators of the injustice and violence. I heard over and over again in my interviews in Colombia the extent to which accompaniment empowers communities and individuals who have been victimized by the violence. Just the presence of outsiders alone gives communities the courage to continue in their struggle for sur vival, the courage to organize, the courage to stay on their lands. It seems to me that empowering and encouraging the victims is that first step that makes a future reconciliation possible, and accompaniment facilitates that.

Truth Telling

A second element is the need for truth telling. The victims need to feel that their stories are being told and heard. I noticed this phenomenon when I was conducting interviews. Community leaders really wanted to tell their stories, and they wanted them to be told to others. Just the act of telling their stories seemed to empower them. It was particularly potent that they had the opportunity to tell their stories to outsiders, because people in their own communities have suffered the same atrocities. Taking to outsiders has the effect of validating to the world what happened and affirming that they have survived.

In his introduction to *Masacres de la Selva*, Ricardo Falla discusses this as the reason he was able to obtain hundreds of testimonies from survivors of the atrocities in Ixcán, Guatemala. People want to tell their stories because, in the telling, they both are announcing the good news that they are alive, and affirming that they will not forget the dead.

> This book has taken on the aim of hundreds of witnesses who want to tell the nation of Guatemala and the whole world: we are alive, incredibly, we are alive.[26]

In affirming they are alive, they are rebuilding their identity, as the world has seen in South Africa.

> In South Africa we see people coming to live in and through their stories. We see people rebuilding their family names word by word as they narrate their painful histories. We are confronted by people returning from the dead in the stories that have been nurtured in the hearts of many people, victims and perpetrators.[27]

Telling the stories also creates a common memory in communities that are often fragmented after so much loss, allowing them to reconstruct communal as well as individual identities.

One study reveals that in the process of telling their stories, victims of violence are able to transform their own history from one of shame and humiliation to one of dignity and virtue. In this way survivors restore their lives and are enabled to move forward.[28] On the other hand, in places where the victims and the survivors have not been acknowledged, "where there has been national amnesia, the effect is a cancer on the society and this is the reason that explains the spiral of violence that the world has seen in former Yugoslavia for centuries and in Rwanda for decades, as obvious examples."[29] What this mean is that, in telling one's story, it is possible to be released from the sense of having endured a history of injustice, and to begin again with a sense of having survived with dignity and virtue.

Listening to the stories of victimized peoples is another aspect of presence. But the accompaniment model, as I have defined it, goes beyond just listening. It also involves speaking the truth of the victimized communities to their own governments and to the outside world. It involves denouncing the abuses, and creating the safe space for communities to denounce the abuses themselves. All of this is part of truth telling, and thus lays the groundwork for a future reconciliation.

26. Falla, *Masacres de la Selva*, ii.

27. Botman, "Narrative Challenges in a Situation of Transition," 37.

28. Montville, "Justice and the Burdens of History," 143.

29. Ibid., 135. He is quoting an interview with Justice Richard Goldstone of the South African Constitutional Court.

Justice

Accompaniment involves work to address the structural causes of violence and injustice. Reconciliation is not possible as long as injustice contin ues—in the form of poverty, displacement, human rights abuses, and vio lent conflict. I have named three ways that an accompaniment mission can address structural causes of injustice: to advocate for policy changes in the missionaries' home countries that are causing the injustice and violence in the first place; to open up the space for local leaders to advocate for changes in their own countries; and to open up a safe space so that com munities can organize and work for their own economic development. In doing so, an accompaniment mission presents nonviolent alternatives to war, thereby witnessing to a biblical call to work for peace. Addressing these structural causes of violence and injustice thus contributes to mak ing a future reconciliation possible.

Restorying

Another element of a reconciliation ministry involves facilitating dialogue among conflicting groups, eventually leading to "restorying" together, meaning creating a new life and a new community where all factions feel they belong. The communities need to be able to create a new narrative, one that has moved beyond the violence and oppression, one that tells the story of overcoming the violence and learning to live together in peace.

We have already seen the seeds of what restorying might look like in the experience of Micoahumado. In no way has full reconciliation taken place, but some seeds have been planted, and, according to the communi ty, that was made possible at least in part through the presence of outside accompaniment. Micoahumado's narrative involves a history of violence, displacement, and poverty, but it now includes a story of organizing, working together, talking with armed groups, and finding a new way for people to stay on their territory. Micoahumado's new story includes the profoundly important roles of the local Catholic Church, especially the community's former pastor Padre Joachim and the Jesuit Padre Francisco, and of international accompaniment in the form of CPT. As missionaries, this is what we hope for: that the resurrection story of a community is linked to our Christian mission work.

Spirituality Based in the Dignity of the Human Person and Respect for Life

The possibility of dialogue presupposes a certain kind of spirituality, one that is based in the dignity of human life and respect for all life, regardless of differences. Without that approach, all sides will approach a dialogue viewing the "other" as enemy rather than as part of one family of God. The reason for the dehumanization of the other is that violent conflict threatens one's own identity. As a result of the violence, the life one has constructed may disappear, and with it one's sense of place and order in the world. Unfortunately, for many peoples of the world, this kind of traumatic loss dominates their memory of their own history, and so their identity also encompasses an enduring sense of injustice.[30] Part of the attempt to maintain one's identity in the face of this sense of injustice often involves a hardening of the boundaries between the self and the other who is seen as the threat. This, in turn, may lead to a dehumanization of the other. Once this happens, both parties to the conflict begin to behave in ways that prolong the conflict. The conflict becomes part of their identity. In such cases the conflict will not be easily resolved unless there is a change in the core sense of identity of one or both parties.

Thus, no future reconciliation can be achieved as long as the other side is dehumanized, or seen as not fully part of the community of God. Padre Francisco pointed out to me that this is one of the most important gifts that CPT brings to Colombia: a spirituality that respects the dignity of all parties.[31] Sandra Milena Rincon, currently the project support coordinator for the CPT Colombia team, also remarked in an interview with me that her work is based in a spirituality of life, and of love of all life.[32] I would add to their comments a reminder that nearly all Christian reflection on morality begins with the first chapter of Genesis: We are created in the image and likeness of God. Christians are grounded in an understanding of the dignity of human life, although that understanding may take different Christians in different directions. I suspect we can all agree, though, that the violations described in chapter 1 of this study are violations of human dignity. Respect for the dignity of life calls us to work to prevent this and, as we have seen, at minimum, international accompaniment diminishes the violence.

30. Montville, "Justice and the Burdens of History," 130–31.

31. Padre Francisco DeRoux, SJ, interview with author.

32. Sandra Milena Rincon, interview with author, December 11, 2008.

A spirituality based on the dignity of all human life must be part of the Good News proclaimed by an accompaniment mission, because with out it, real dialogue among equals is not possible.

Ecumenical and Interfaith Action

A spirituality based in respect for all life involves ecumenism—or, in multi-faith contexts, interfaith dialogue and action. It is no secret that many violent conflicts have religious differences at their core, and often this is mixed with some kind of nationalistic political thinking. Religion and nationalism are a lethal mixture that has led to violence in Sudan, Israel/Palestine, the Balkans, Northern Ireland, and elsewhere. Plenty of writers have suggested that the problem is with religion, and that if we could neutralize religion, the world would be a safer place. Other writers have contradicted this, saying that the problem is not with religion, but with religion that has been distorted. What is certain is that in areas where seeds of conflict already exist—such as in areas with extreme poverty, vast income differences among various groups, or marginalization of certain groups—the last thing needed are competing religious groups. It is for this reason that a theology of mission that places conversion to Christianity, or to a particular Christian denomination, at its center is simply inappropri ate in a zone of violent conflict.

An ecumenical, or interfaith, witness among missionaries *is* appro priate in a conflict zone and is part of a ministry of reconciliation. CPT is a Christian organization with multi-faith membership. Its teams are comprised of members of a full range of Christian confessions, serving together with members of other faith traditions. Because Colombia is a predominantly Christian country, ecumenism is important; in places like Israel/Palestine, where the population is comprised of many faiths, I be lieve that interfaith teams are appropriate, and part of the work of those teams is figuring out how a Christian witness can coexist in the same com munity with witnesses from other faiths. In addition to coexisting in the same accompaniment mission, another way to realize an interfaith vision is to develop liturgies and public prayers and actions together with spiri tual leaders from a variety of faith traditions.

Liturgy and Prayer

Liturgy and prayer, especially those that involve the healing of memories and the telling of a community's story, is also an element of a reconciliation ministry. The healing of memory is part of what strengthens the victim and enables her to forgive and reach out in a process of dialogue with the perpetrator. Liturgies that name the suffering, such as the one conducted by Padre Raphael each year in Tiquisio, are part of the public acknowledgement of the truth of what happened, and thus are part of the healing of the victim. Liturgies can also play a role in creating a new story: the liturgy can name the suffering, but can also facilitate the community coming together in new relationships and a new life together. I will discuss this aspect of accompaniment more fully in the next section of this chapter.

Prayerful public actions, in the streets or in front of the seats of power, are also part of this ministry, because they publicly acknowledge the truth of what happened and can thus be healing for the victim. One example of the power of such public liturgical expressions took place in Chile, beginning in 1983, during the Pinochet years. A group of Roman Catholic nuns, priests, and laypeople began to participate in public, liturgical actions against torture. These actions took place in front of public buildings that were symbolic of the regime's policies of torture, including the courts, jails, government buildings, and the headquarters of the media. Members of the movement would appear as if out of nowhere, unfurling banners and often blocking traffic. The actions would include songs and litanies of protest against torture, often naming the victims. Members of the movement, called *El Movimiento Contra la Tortura Sebastián Acevedo*, were frequently beaten and arrested. One writer describes the power of these public liturgical activities:

> Suddenly the silence and invisibility under which the torture apparatus operates are shattered, interrupting its power. In an astonishing ritual transformation, clandestine torture centers are revealed to the passersby for what they are, as if a veil covering the building were abruptly taken away. The complicity of other sectors of the government and society is laid bare for all to see. The entire torture system suddenly appears on a city street.[33]

One of the leaders described these public rituals as forming a "new conception of society," which is attested to by the presence of the

33. Cavanaugh, *Torture and Eucharist*, 275.

demonstrators. "They can beat us or attack us with water and gases, but there we are to anticipate this new society."[34] Creation of a "new society" is exactly the way I have described the nature of reconciliation. These kinds of public rituals anticipate and even help to usher in the future that com munities long for.

As we have seen, international accompaniment of these local actions would likely reduce the risk of retaliation against the participants, and in crease the likelihood that the actions would be publicized internationally, which could affect perceptions as well as government policies, both inter nally and externally. Public actions, such as demonstrations or a ritualized naming of the violence, are a particular charism of CPT.

Members of Christian Peacemaker Teams and other local
organizations hold a prayer service at the border wall between Arizona
and Mexico to remember migrants who have died crossing the border.

34. Ibid.

Christian Peacemaker Teams, along with members of an accompanied Palestinian community, bless the planting of new olive trees after their olive grove was vandalized by nearby Israeli settlers.

Healing From Trauma

Dealing with the trauma of victims is needed in a zone of violence but one that most missionaries are ill equipped to handle. Indeed, the reality is that most members of CPT have to try and manage their own trauma, which develops as a result of being exposed to levels of violence and abuse that many have not encountered in their home countries. Many of the steps discussed above—including the presence of outside accompaniers, public truth telling, and healing liturgies—are part of a trauma healing ministry. But there is more that could be done by trained professionals working with individual victims who are particularly paralyzed by trauma. An accompaniment ministry that includes working with victims (as well as missionaries) to overcome their trauma is important in a zone of violent conflict, and can contribute to enabling and empowering victims to take the first steps toward a future reconciliation.

In this section I have named the elements that need to be in place in order to make possible a future reconciliation: these include truth telling, eliminating the structural causes of injustice, forgiveness on the part of the victim, repentance on the part of the perpetrator, dialogue among all groups, and a restorying that involves communities developing a new group narrative that embraces all sides and brings them to new life to gether. The final reconciliation can only be accomplished by God and thus is beyond human activity. We cannot make it happen. But we can take concrete steps in that direction, and in this section I have indicated what some of those steps might be. An accompaniment mission in a zone of violent conflict will work to lay the groundwork for a future reconciliation that is ultimately beyond us.

LITURGY, PRAYER, AND CONTEMPLATION

In the accompaniment model of mission, liturgy and public prayer are the means by which overt proclamation of the Gospel takes place. They are also crucial for a ministry of reconciliation. Public prayer should include ecumenical prayer that witnesses to Christian unity, and, where appropri ate, interfaith services. Local salvation history, meaning the community's own story, should be included in the liturgical celebration. Further, the contemplative processes of listening and relationship building are foun dational to the accompaniment paradigm, of which companionship and solidarity are key components.

Public Prayer and Liturgy

I noted earlier the value of public ritual for a ministry of reconciliation. More generally, prayer and liturgy, both public and private, sustain and empower the ministry of accompaniment, and for Christians public prayer is the primary way in which Jesus Christ is proclaimed in word and in ritual.

Furthermore, recent studies indicate that liturgy has a special role to play in contexts of extreme violence. Conflict threatens identity. Through conflict, people and sometimes entire communities lose members of their families, their homes, their livelihoods, their religious places, their cul tural monuments. The life one has constructed may disappear, and with it one's sense of place in the world. Ritual can heal fragmented identities, and protect one's identity from fragmenting, particularly when one's identity is connected to the ritual in the first place.[35] Returning to the ritual can

35. Schirch, *Ritual and Symbol in Peacebuilding*, 130–31.

restore one's sense of order, when order has been shattered. In my own case, after surviving a violent attack, my first desire was to attend Mass. I understand now that participating in the ritual helped me to return to the core of my identity, and to see that ultimately the sacred cannot be destroyed.

Prayer and liturgy play an important role in the work of CPT. Most CPT teams meet daily for prayer and reflection as a community. In addition, in Colombia, we can find numerous examples of CPT members publicly praying, with families or communities at risk, and with armed groups. For example, in an October 2001 report, CPT member William Payne reports praying with a group of guerrilla members and leading them in scripture reflection:

> We also met with a large group of imprisoned people who are linked with the guerrillas. They invited us to lead them in a morning of reflection on Jesus' message of nonviolence. They were very open to our message, though many of them expressed disbelief in its possibility . . . The only thing we have to offer here is the crazy idea that Jesus introduced—that we need to abandon the use of violence. It does not seem logical to do so, but the logic of violence does not seem to be helping the situation either. "Love your enemy," Jesus said. How do we try to explain that to someone whose enemy killed her brother?[36]

Another CPT member, Carol Foltz Spring, describes a later incident when paramilitary forces stopped a public transportation bus full of unarmed civilians: "Scott and I opened an impromptu vigil, praying and singing, 'Nada te turbe' ('Let nothing distress you')."[37]

During my most recent time with the CPT Colombia team, in December 2008, a CPT neighbor was murdered, and paramilitary forces were suspected. Maritza Gutierez Hoyos, wife of CPT member Pierre Schantz, organized a public prayer vigil led by the local Catholic priest on the front steps of the murdered man's house. The entire CPT team attended, along with many local human rights workers. On occasion local partners ask CPT in Colombia to help with the planning of ecumenical public prayer services to coincide with large events or gatherings of human rights workers.

The willingness of many members of CPT to engage in public prayer and ritual in the midst of violent conflict and suffering provides a healing

---

36. Payne, *Colombia: Looking for the Prophets*, para. 5.

37. Spring, *Colombia: Claimed Collaboration*, para. 8.

presence. It is a way to proclaim Christianity without an agenda of conver
sion. In this way, as suggested by Suess in the previous chapter, the mis
sionary offers her faith with humility, through her presence and through
her prayer.

Contemplation

Contemplative practices are foundational to a ministry of accompani
ment. Indeed, in my view the ministry of international protective ac
companiment itself is a contemplative practice. Christian contemplation
has its biblical basis in the traditional interpretation of the Mary/Martha
story in Luke, chapter 10. In this story, Jesus rebukes Martha for being
too busy, and not stopping to listen and be present to Jesus. Mary sits at
the feet of Jesus and listens to what he has to say. Jesus tells us that there
is no need to be distracted; there is need of only one thing, and that is
to listen. Contemplation is listening: listening to the interior voice of the
divine, being present to that voice, and also listening and being present to
the voice of God in others. In contemplation, presence is more important
than frenzied activity, and presence is the heart of international protective
accompaniment.

The passage in Luke is not saying that there is something wrong with
activity. We all have activities that we need to accomplish, and prayer itself
is an activity. This passage reminds its readers that we must listen first, be
fore acting, and that our action develops from our listening. It is through
listening that we understand what our actions need to be.

A complementary biblical narrative is Matthew chapter 25. In this
story Jesus identifies himself with the "least" of God's people: the poor, the
prisoner, the oppressed, the marginalized of his time. When Christians
respond to the needs of the marginalized, we are responding to the needs
of Jesus. Thus, listening to the marginalized is a way of sitting at the feet
of Jesus. So when we accompany communities at risk of violence, we are
accompanying Jesus. And when we listen to those communities articulate
their needs, we are listening to Jesus. When we respond to those needs by
our presence and by our witness, we are serving Jesus.

An interesting side note here is that much of the contemporary liter
ature on the ministry of spiritual direction, itself a contemplative ministry,
describes it as "spiritual accompaniment." The spiritual director is the ac
companier, while the directee is the person being accompanied. Spiritual
accompaniment consists of several components analogous to a mission of
international protective accompaniment:

- It is based in relationship, companionship, and presence.
- It calls upon the accompanier to witness his or her faith to the accompanied.
- The accompanier recognizes God in the accompanied.
- The accompanier never imposes anything on the accompanied, because even if the accompanier believes she can improve things for the accompanied, God's grace can do so much more.
- Spiritual accompaniment proceeds based on dialogue between the accompanied and the accompanier.
- The purpose of spiritual accompaniment is to call forth the fullness of life in the accompanied.[38]

Thus we can approach international protective accompaniment as a means to bring forth the fullness of life in the exterior world, whereas spiritual accompaniment is a means to bring about the fullness of life in the interior world. Both are necessary and complementary if life is to flourish.

Although each of the above five elements of accompaniment are equally important, the entire praxis is founded on dialogue.

DIALOGUE

Dialogue, or conversation, is foundational to all of the elements of accompaniment activity, and begins with presence and companionship. Future reconciliation can only happen when all sides of a conflict engage in a conversation. Although dialogue is integral to all aspects of an accompaniment mission, it is worth placing it in a separate category, to emphasize its importance. The other elements of accompaniment cannot exist without dialogue.

CONCLUSION: ACCOMPANIMENT AS PROPHETIC DIALOGUE

In the *prophetic dialogue* approach, the starting point for mission is dialogue. Dialogue is imitation of our Trinitarian, Creator God. God pours out God's self in a creative act of goodness, designing the universe and conceiving of men and women in God's own likeness. True dialogue also

---

38. Louf, *Grace Can Do More*, ix–39.

requires a a kind of self-emptying, because presence, involving listening, learning, and relationship-building, is not focused first on the needs of the self, but rather the needs of the other. But to be prophetic, the missionary must also proclaim Christian values and convey a commitment to a future Reign of God that is not yet here but that all Christians are called to seek.

The practice of international accompaniment is both prophetic and dialogical on every level. An accompaniment mission is initiated through dialogue and a mutual decision between accompanied and accompaniers from the outset. A presence of accompaniment in a zone of violent conflict also makes dialogue possible on another level, because the presence of outsiders enables dialogue with armed actors, lowering the risk of violence against the communities. Dialogue with armed actors is also a deeply pro phetic, nonviolent witness to the dignity of all human life. Accompaniers, through their presence and relationship with highly vulnerable popula tions, risk their own lives in a prophetic witness to the value of the lives of others.

This chapter has correlated the conclusions of chapter 2 with the conclusions of chapter 3. In other words, I have taken the elements of in ternational protective accompaniment and placed them within an accom paniment model of Christian mission. We have seen that all the elements of accompaniment—witness and proclamation, liturgy, contemplation, and prayer, working for justice, peace, and integrity of creation, encultura tion, the ministry of reconciliation, and dialogue—are present in the work of international protective accompaniment and specifically in the work of CPT. I am thus suggesting that international protective accompaniment is one model, or example, of an appropriate Christian mission for our time.

We have also seen that doing international protective accompani ment well, in a way that is life-giving for the communities, requires deep theological and spiritual formation of the missionaries, especially in a spirituality based on the dignity of the human person, on an understand ing of God as accompanying us in our suffering, and, for Christians, on identifying one's suffering with the suffering of Jesus on the Cross.

Christian Peacemaker Teams and the other accompaniment groups are small and poorly funded. What would happen if we placed a thousand well-trained accompaniers in a conflict zone? We have seen dramatic re sults in some of the small communities where they have been present. Current practice among mission organizations often involves withdraw ing from an area when conflict breaks out. In that case, the message to the community is this: We can be with you in times of peace, but in times of danger, we leave, and we take our faith with us. I suggest that withdrawing is a poor witness to Christianity. In this chapter I have provided a mission praxis that, while entailing some risk, enables missionaries to stay with their communities and do constructive work in times of violent conflict. As such, I have outlined a new paradigm for mission in zones of violent conflict.

5

Accompaniment as Peacebuilding

*May the Spirit that marvelously transforms the bread and the wine
into the body and blood of Christ, the Son of the Virgin Mary, also
transform all of us into instruments of peace, and into prophets of
prayer, truth, justice, and love.*

—Most Reverend Luis Augusto Castro Quiroga,
Colombia, during a conference at the University of
Notre Dame, April 2008

In the 1980s, Roman Catholic Bishop Jorge Leonardo Gomez Serna of
the Diocese of Magangue, Colombia, began to experience high levels of
violence among competing armed groups within his diocese. Both Tiqu
isio and Micoahumado are located within the Diocese of Magangue. As a
result, Bishop Gomez Serna began to seek out dialogue with members of
armed groups, in the hopes of diminishing the violence and humanizing
the conflict. In 1987, he initiated what came to be called *dialogos pasto
rales,* or pastoral dialogues. These dialogues consist of direct discussions
by church leadership with armed actors to find ways to preserve life and
dignity in communities affected by the violence. In 1992 then-President
Cesar Gaviria Trujillo proclaimed that citizens were not permitted to
take up direct dialogue with armed groups. Defying the president, Bishop
Gomez Serna wrote: "The government can prohibit all the dialogues it
wishes, but not those that I undertake as a pastor of the church."[1]

---

1. Lederach, "Long Journey Back to Humanity," 37.

The Colombian constitutional court later affirmed that pastoral dialogues cannot be prohibited by the state. These often-dangerous pastoral dialogues have taken place across Colombia, and in some cases, such as in Micoahumado, have led to community dialogues and zones of peace in certain territories. The dialogues represent peacebuilding on the front lines.

Separate from the work of Christian Peacemaker Teams, local faith-based actors, especially the Catholic Church, are engaged in what is frequently called "pastoral accompaniment" in Colombia and around the globe. The pastoral dialogues described above are an element of pastoral accompaniment. Pastoral accompaniment takes place at the level of communities affected by violence and is aimed at transforming the situation from one of armed conflict to one of restored community. Through pastoral accompaniment, Catholic leaders seek to reaffirm the humanity of both victims and armed actors; restore families and communities broken apart by violence; work for social justice as the foundation for peace; and, perhaps most significantly, dialogue with armed actors. CPT adds the dimension of outside accompaniment, in areas where it is present, to work that is already happening within the local churches.

Such conflict transformation work led by faith-based actors on the front lines of conflict zones is one element of an emerging theology and praxis of peacebuilding. This work is taking place not only in Colombia, but also in other war-torn countries around the world. The aims and methods of peacebuilding are similar to the aims and goals of mission work in a zone of violent conflict, as outlined in this book. In this chapter I suggest that the two disciplines, mission and peacebuilding, should be brought together, so that each can inform and enrich the other.

Like mission, *peacebuilding* is both a theology and a praxis. Unlike mission, peacebuilding is an emerging discipline that is developing in the context of protracted conflicts, such as the one in Colombia, that are a twentieth- and twenty-first-century phenomenon. Peacebuilding comprises a range of topics not addressed by theological writings on the ethics of the use of force. These topics include conflict prevention, conflict management and transformation, and post-conflict reconciliation. Peacebuilding thus focuses on actors, relationships, and practices ranging from before armed conflict breaks out until after the overt violence has ended. Its aim is to address the underlying causes of the conflict so that violence will not reemerge or take other forms. As such, it is much more than simply working to negotiate an end to overt violence. Peacebuilding aims to restore relationships and communities. According to R. Scott Appleby, Director of Notre Dame's Kroc Institute for International Peace Studies, peacebuilders "strive to address all phases of these protracted conflicts, in which pre-violence, violence, and post-violence periods are difficult to differentiate."[2] He has also observed that at the heart of peacebuilding is the intentional building, at every level of society, of relationships dedi cated to nonviolent transformation of conflict, the pursuit of social justice, and the creation of cultures of sustainable peace.[3]

A milestone in this emerging discipline took place in April twenty-five years after publication of the US Catholic Bishops' peace pastoral, *The Challenge of Peace*, when more than 275 Catholic theolo gians, bishops, pastors, and grassroots peacebuilders from around the world gathered at Notre Dame University for a *Conference on the Future of Catholic Peacebuilding*. The Catholic Peacebuilding Network (CPN) and eighteen co-sponsors organized the conference. Founded in and spearheaded by Notre Dame's Kroc Institute and Catholic Relief Ser vices, CPN is a coalition of academics and practitioners, clergy and laity, that seeks to enhance the study and practice of Catholic peacebuilding. CPN convenes, on a regular basis, a diverse range of people engaged in the study and practice of conflict prevention, conflict transformation, and post-conflict reconciliation.

The Notre Dame conference brought together theologians and peacebuilders from war-torn areas around the globe. This type of gather ing had never been attempted before. It is for that reason that it is worth exploring, in depth, the themes generated by the conference presentations. Participants included an interdisciplinary group of scholars, Church lead ers, and peacebuilding specialists from Church institutions and Catholic lay organizations. Many participants came from countries affected by con flict, including delegations from Mindanao in the Philippines, the Great Lakes region of Africa, and Colombia—three areas of special focus for CPN. Nine Catholic bishops participated from these areas, as well as from Nigeria and the United States. The conference underscored that, in a world divided by poverty, ethnic and religious rivalry, and armed conflict, it is crucial to articulate a coherent foundational theology and effective praxis. Foundational theology refers to the key ideas in Catholic faith tradition that support ending violence and building up a peaceful world. Effective

2. Appleby, "Peacebuilding and Catholicism," 3.
3. Appleby, "Many Dimensions of Catholic Peacebuilding," 2.

praxis refers to the methods that faith-based practitioners of peace might employ in order to attain the peaceful world envisioned by our faith.

Conference speakers stressed that from facilitating negotiations between the government and rebels in Colombia, Burundi, and Uganda; to promoting reconciliation between Catholics and Muslims in the Philippines and Nigeria; to providing humanitarian assistance, reducing civilian casualties, and providing pastoral messages of peace and courage in almost every conflict around the world, the Catholic community plays a critical role.

The conference was about theology and ethics, as they are informed by and inform practice. Many of the papers presented at the conference were edited and published in a major book on Catholic peacebuilding in 2010.[4] A central message was the need for greater appreciation and awareness that the vocation of peacebuilding is central to the life and mission of the Catholic Church. For example, in his final plenary presentation, Archibishop John Onaiyekan of Nigeria stressed that peacebuilding is a natural project for the Church of God, and should be in the mainstream of the work Catholics do.

On behalf of the Catholic Peacebuilding Network, I wrote the (unpublished) conference report. I attended every plenary session, took extensive notes, listened to the tapes of workshops I could not attend, and read every paper. Looking at the conference as a whole, I found that the presentations highlighted five main categories of peacebuilding activity: respect for human rights; poverty alleviation and just economic development; interreligious dialogue and action; pastoral accompaniment and conflict transformation; and the practice of reconciliation. The conference highlighted the many fine activities of church actors in conflict zones, much of which was previously not well-publicized. However, the conference and subsequent written materials did not include the work of the international protective accompaniment groups. That is an omission which this chapter seeks to rectify. In my view international protective accompaniment complements and strengthens the work of local faith-based peacebuilders, and should be viewed as one of a number of effective peacebuilding tools.

The following pages describe each of the five main categories of peacebuilding activity in more detail, illustrating how international protective accompaniment as described in the previous chapters of this book, can be viewed as one model, or example, of a peacebuilding praxis.

4. Schreiter et al., *Peacebuilding*.

RESPECT FOR HUMAN RIGHTS
AND HUMAN DIGNITY

Lack of respect for basic human dignity is what leads to violence and war, stated Burundian Archbishop Joachim Ntahondereye, sharing from his experience with the refugee crisis in Burundi. Echoing many other expe rienced peacebuilders at the conference, Archbishop Ntahondereye said that building a culture of respect for human dignity addresses the root causes of violence.

> We have to denounce the violation of human rights and to defend them, but we have also to promote them daily, through our personal behavior and through the way we treat our fellow human beings.[5]

Building peace involves building a culture of peace, and this begins with respect for human dignity.

Respect for the dignity of human life is at the core of Catholic teach ing, and is also a key theme of international protective accompaniment. The most significant dimension of an accompaniment program is pres ence that is grounded in relationship. What I found in my experience, and what leaders in conflict-affected communities confirmed in chapter that the presence of outsiders validates and affirms the dignity of persons who have suffered unspeakable tragedies. In affirming their dignity, ac companiers affirm their efforts to remain on their territory and recon struct their shattered lives.

Furthermore, a spirituality of accompaniment that is grounded in respect for the dignity of each person is, by its nature, respectful of the dig nity of people on all sides of the conflict. This posture of respect encour ages those in the midst of conflict to seek nonviolent alternatives, such as dialogue and negotiation. It provides a witness that helps make possible dialogues between and among all sides.

JUST ECONOMIC DEVELOPMENT

Although Latin Americans are not the poorest peoples of the world, they have the highest degree of income inequality, noted conference presenter Laura Vargas, director of the Comisión Episcopal de Acción Social in Peru. Poverty itself, she added, is a mass violation of human rights, because

---

5 Lamberty, "Conference on the Future of Catholic Peacebuilding," 8.

people have the right to those things that allow life to flourish: food, clean water, medical care, education. She also pointed out that the poor tend to be the ones who suffer the most during violent conflicts, because they are already living on the margins, and so when their food supply or income is disrupted, they cannot recover easily. In order to stop creating poverty-related victims of violent conflict, income inequality must be addressed through development programs that directly benefit the poor.[6] This is consistent with what we have already learned about the benefits of accompaniment programs: accompaniment enables people whose lives have been disrupted by conflict to stay on their territories, rather than displacing, and then to initiate economic development programs.

One obstacle to generating development programs that benefit the poor is a common model of natural resources exploitation used in developing countries. This model of economic development, rather than benefiting vulnerable communities, is frequently a cause of conflict, and that in turn makes them more vulnerable. Multiple presenters in various sessions of the 2008 conference pointed to the relationship between natural resource exploitation and violent conflict. Fr. Ferdinand Muhigirwa, SJ, of the Centre d'Etudes Pour l'Action Sociale (CEPAS) in the Democratic Republic of Congo, described the problem as two-fold. Corruption and poor organizing among artisanal miners or farmers permits rebel or guerrilla groups to exploit natural resources illegally in order to fund their movements. In addition, transnational corporations push out small-scale development projects and create mega-projects that do not benefit the poor. Martha Ines Romero, from Catholic Relief Services Colombia and Pax Christi International, noted that the same dynamic is taking place within the Colombian agriculture sector, where transnational companies are developing large swaths of land and converting them to palm and other products for use in biofuels, at the expense of developing indigenous methods of production that would benefit those who have traditionally survived off the land.[7] Indeed, we have already seen the effects of extractive industries on the communities featured in this study, Micoahumado and Tiquisio.

Fr. Muhigirwa suggested that solutions should include leadership training and community organizing for small-scale miners and agricultural workers, and national and international advocacy. These are some of the same solutions suggested in my international protective accompaniment

6. Ibid., 9–10.
7. Ibid., 10.

model, and what we have seen is that accompaniment actualizes these ideas. A good accompaniment program collaborates with local organiza tions to open up the space for community organizing, the development of democratic processes, and leadership development. It also advocates for the rights of the vulnerable with the national and international authorities who control their fate. These solutions have been successful in Micoahu mado and Tiquisio, the two communities studied in chapter 2.

INTERRELIGIOUS DIALOGUE AND ACTION

Adherents of *all* major religions, with no exception, have engaged in mas sive and systematic violence in the name of their faiths, against other be lievers and non-believers and even against their own fellow believers, often with the official sanction and encouragement of their hierarchy, noted Georgetown University theologian Peter Phan.[8] Because the interaction between different religious traditions plays such a central role in fostering armed conflict, it must also play an indispensable role in peacebuilding.

Numerous conference presentations focused on the importance of interreligious dialogue and cooperation in fostering peace. Often religious leadership is the only force within society that retains credibility with the people affected by the violence, and because religious leaders live close to, and in relationship with, the people, they are also frequently closer to the needs and aspirations of the people than are governments or rebel groups. Phan and others suggested that religious leaders manage to come together to work for peace when conflict breaks out, rather than fostering discord, only when they have a prior history of working together. This suggests that in areas where conflict is endemic or where there is a high potential for conflict, religious leadership can begin to become part of the solution by finding ways to work together and collaborate, for the good of the com munities they are in, before there are overt signs of violence.

A good accompaniment program is itself a witness to ecumenical and/or interreligious collaboration. In chapter 2 we saw that the ecumeni cal nature of the CPT program was considered especially valuable in a conflict zone precisely because it embodies and witnesses to the value of cooperation and teamwork. In a more interfaith context, that cooperation extends to members of all religious traditions. Interreligious collabora tion need not be based on common agreement about religious truths. As Christians, we are grounded in our belief in the intrinsic dignity of each

8. Ibid., 12.

person, and so we must recognize that our lives are bound up with each other, no matter the religious tradition, and that we are co-creators of the new world, free of violence, that we are all seeking.

PASTORAL ACCOMPANIMENT
AND CONFLICT TRANSFORMATION

In Catholic majority countries, and even those where the Church enjoys a significant portion of a plurality, the ecclesiology and structure of the hierarchy places the Catholic leadership in a unique position for peace-building, observed John Paul Lederach, a Mennonite scholar and foremost expert on conflict transformation, who teaches at the University of Notre Dame. Activities aimed at conflict transformation include everything from forms of advocacy, observation, conciliation, facilitation, and mediation between armed groups and the government; to local parish initiatives to protect and mediate the release of family members captured in the fray of armed conflict. From his experience working with Catholic leaders around the globe who are located in situations of armed conflict, Lederach has found that they most often describe their conflict transformation activities using the concepts of accompaniment, presence, and space. Catholic leaders accompany individuals, communities, and processes through their presence, creating spaces for peace.[9]

Although Church leaders are often involved at the top levels of discussion and negotiation, this work of conflict transformation in the form of pastoral accompaniment takes place primarily at the level of the communities affected by the violence. Accompaniment is aimed at transforming the situation from armed conflict to restored community. Through pastoral accompaniment, Catholic leaders seek to reaffirm the humanity of both victims and armed actors, restore families and communities broken apart by violence, work for social justice as the foundation for peace, and, perhaps most significantly, dialogue with armed actors. The term "armed actors" refers to any of the individuals or groups, official or unofficial, who have taken up arms and are part of the violent conflict. Catholic leaders pursue dialogue with armed actors as part of their pastoral duty to accompany the victims, as well as to find a way out of the unceasing violence. In this way pastoral accompaniment is a means to prevent conflict

9. Ibid., 14.

from breaking out again sometime in the future, because it addresses the root causes of violence.[10]

Lederach describes the work of local church leaders as "pastoral ac companiment." In chapter 2 we saw that this work of pastoral accompani ment by the local church and by human rights groups was made possible by the presence of international accompaniment. The internationals pro vide an umbrella of safety for local pastoral and human rights workers, themselves frequently under threat of violence, which enables the local workers to carry on with their own mission of accompaniment.

In an earlier work, Lederach wrote that, based on his decades of ex perience, transcending violence "is forged by the capacity to generate, mo bilize, and build the moral imagination."[11] What Lederach is naming the "moral imagination" is mobilized, held together, and sustained through the practice of four disciplines.

> Stated simply, the moral imagination requires the capacity to imagine ourselves in a web of relationships that includes our enemies; the ability to sustain a paradoxical curiosity that em braces complexity without reliance on dualistic polarity; the fundamental belief in and pursuit of the creative act; and the acceptance of the inherent risk of stepping into the mystery of the unknown that lies beyond the far too familiar landscape of violence.[12]

The capacity he refers to is the ability to respond to everyday violence, fear, and intimidation in ways that transcend, rather than foment, that violence. Such responses include the ability to transcend the "us vs. them" mentality that characterizes conflict zones, and to work toward a new world that is inclusive of everyone. Such transcendence is itself a creative act, especially in contexts such as war-torn Colombia, where violence is endemic, youth have witnessed little else, and they believe that they need to join one armed group or another in order to "resolve their lives," as Padre Rafael stated so succinctly.

I am suggesting that the practice of international accompaniment can contribute to creating the conditions and capacities that Lederach describes. An example will illustrate the point. In the fall of 2006 in Colombia accompanying a group of artisan miners who had experi enced violence, intimidation, and threats from armed groups—especially

10. Ibid., 14–15.

11. Lederach, *Moral Imagination*, 5.

12. Ibid.

the Colombian armed forces and paramilitary groups—after organizing themselves into a labor union and fighting for their right to continue to maintain their traditional way of life and run their small mining business-es, rather than allow a large transnational mining operation to take over. After a member of the union was accused of being a guerrilla and shot by the Colombian armed forces, the miners gathered high in the mountains to decide how to respond. Christian Peacemaker Teams was called to ac-company their process and I was part of that team. When we arrived, the miners were upset and restless, but soon after we arrived they decided on a plan to march down the mountain, hold peaceful demonstrations in Santa Rosa, and ask for negotiations with the Colombian government. Their leaders told me that it was CPT's presence that calmed them down and encouraged them to seek solutions that presented an alternative to violence.

The author accompanies a demonstration of miners
in Santa Rosa, Colombia, 2006.

What we have seen is that the presence of eyes from the outside provides some crucial but intangible elements that help enable people to think outside the box and seek alternatives. What outside accompaniment provides is difficult to measure, but it seems to center on two different kinds of things. First, it reduces the fear, because vulnerable communities believe that armed groups are less likely to kill when there are internation als present. This may or may not be true, but the perception is key, and it seems to open up the space for communities to think about alternatives. Second, by their presence among groups that have suffered unspeakable tragedy, outside accompaniers validate the dignity and life projects of these groups. This encourages the groups to offer the best of themselves, rather than reverting to old patterns.

It is clear that many other factors are in play in cases where violence is transcended. In particular, Lederach mentions the importance of ac companiment by the local church, and we saw that as well in the work of *Programa*. As noted above, Martha Ines Romero of Catholic Relief Ser vices Colombia also addressed this topic at the conference, emphasizing the importance of community-based pastoral accompaniment over and above top-down approaches to conflict transformation. She noted these dimensions of Catholic Church-based accompaniment: The permanent presence of pastoral workers (priests or lay people); active listening as a way to allow the victims to testify to what happened to them, thereby retrieving the truth of what happened; mediation and finding solutions through dialogue with armed actors; and promoting a message of hope to accompany endangered and affected communities. Ms. Romero testified that, in her experience, these local approaches, community by community, are what will lead to a comprehensive solution to the conflict.[13]

The presence of international accompaniment has helped to make this community-based pastoral work possible by diminishing the vulner ability of pastoral workers, many of whom have been subjected to threats, kidnapping, intimidation, and violence. In short, I am suggesting that the presence of international eyes from the outside helps to create the condi tions that give rise to the moral imagination, and that this, in turn, con tributes to transcending conflict and creating alternatives.

POST-CONFLICT RECONSTRUCTION
AND RECONCILIATION

Chapter 4 discussed the ministry of reconciliation extensively, noting that it is at the heart of how we understand mission today, and that internation al accompaniment contributes to creating the conditions where reconcili ation may take place. Robert Schreiter, who has written extensively about

13. Lamberty, "Report: Conference on the Future of Catholic Peacebuilding,"

reconciliation as mission, also presented at the Notre Dame conference on reconciliation as peacebuilding. Reconciliation must be seen both as a *goal* and a *process*, he said. As a goal, reconciliation is aimed at a state of biblical *shalom*, which means living in "right relationship" with God, our fellow human beings, and with all of creation. As a process, reconciliation requires the practice of mercy, which concretely entails the practices of healing and forgiveness.[14] Healing involves acknowledging loss, lamenting and grieving for those who will now no longer share one's life, and looking for ways to move forward, Schreiter continued. Violence denies basic human dignity, and in so doing wrests away from us part of our humanity. We are treated as objects to which others can be indifferent. Healing can thus be defined as restoring the humanity and dignity of the victims of violence.

Forgiveness between individuals is generally understood as the victim giving up resentment against the perpetrator, followed by restoration of the social bond between the two. Social forgiveness involves one group forgiving another, and is marked by three steps: Acknowledgement, or truth telling, is taking responsibility for having inflicted pain, and is key to overcoming alienation and beginning to build a new relationship. Following acknowledgement, there must be some ritual of apology. Finally, there must be an offer of atonement, which may involve reparations, special new relationships, or legal guarantees to prevent future injustices.

Significantly, Schreiter's comments about the elements required for reconciliation bear strong resemblance to Lederach's comments about the elements of a moral imagination. Both understand that the goal is a new creation that exists beyond the current imagination, one that requires the development of new capacities in order to overcome the pain of past wrongs.

Without repeating the in-depth discussion of reconciliation in chapter 4, a key point is that reconciliation must begin with the victim and depends upon empowerment of the victim. The victim must feel that the truth is being told and justice is being done before he or she is ready to being a process of forgiveness. The presence of international accompaniment can help to facilitate this process, by enabling the victims of violence to reconstruct their shattered lives, plan for the future, and remain on their territories.

Conference presenters also took up the concept of political reconciliation. Daniel Philpott argued that six practices express reconciliation

14. Ibid., 17.

concretely in the context of politics: building socially just institutions, acknowledgment, reparations, punishment, apology, and forgiveness. Truth and reconciliation commissions, such as the one that was formed in South Africa after the end of the apartheid regime, address political reconciliation. Political reconciliation is necessary because, in many cases, the state is the wrongdoer. However, the existence of failed, or predatory, states renders reconciliation at the individual and community level even more vital for building an enduring peace, because individual and com munity reconciliation can help to realize political reconciliation, by creat ing an environment where victims feel empowered to step forward and tell their stories.[15] In other words, reconciliation at the state level is vital, and requires truth and reconciliation commissions, but, and echoing Martha Ines Romero, it does not replace reconciliation processes at the commu nity level, and these are the processes that international accompaniment can help to facilitate.

CONCLUSION

Peacebuilding requires the capacity to imagine peace. Although top-down, political resolutions are important for putting an end to overt vio lent conflict, community-based solutions that both address the root causes of the violence and find ways to bring opposing sides together are what bring about a comprehensive solution. A government-negotiated end to the conflict is not what makes it possible for former enemies to live and work together in the same village. For that to happen, a much more pro found movement needs to take place. And without such a movement, the violence can return at any time. Peacebuilding demands that individuals and communities on all sides of a conflict be able to imagine life together, without the violence. Although many factors contribute to creating the conditions that allow this movement to take place, we have seen that in ternational accompaniment is one such factor.

Colombian Jesuit Father Francisco DeRoux told me in a personal in terview that he was struck, during his time facilitating dialogues between armed groups and communities that were victims of violence, that all sides had a vision for a better Colombia. Recognizing this will be the start ing point for imagining a new Colombia, where everyone has a place and no one is excluded. This new place would be the fulfillment of Isaiah

15. Ibid., 18–19.

They shall beat their swords into plowshares, and their spears into pruning hooks; nation shall not lift up sword against nation, neither shall they learn war any more.[16]

16. Isa 2:4 NRSV.

Conclusion

Building a Just Peace

A FEW YEARS AGO, in Guatemala, a local human rights worker, who is indigenous, recounted to me his memories of foreign Catholic missionaries in his town. He recalled that the townspeople were very close to the missionaries, and nearly everyone worshipped at the Catholic Church. Then, in the 1980s, the town was threatened by guerrilla and military confrontations. At that point, the missionaries departed. "What good is your Christianity to us?" this man asked me. The townspeople were faced with difficult choices about leaving their lands and becoming refugees, or staying put under threat of violence and death. They suffered enormous losses during the decades-long conflict.

We can all understand the fear that would cause missionaries to depart, but their departure highlighted the very different worlds of the missionaries and the receiving communities. The message conveyed by their departure is that the life of a missionary is more valuable than the lives of an indigenous community in Guatemala. The missionaries left the people to suffer alone, witnessing to a God who abandons them in their darkest hour.

"Please don't leave us alone," was the principal message of the community leaders I interviewed in Colombia. The victims of violations, abuse, and war, cry out to Christians as images of Jesus on the Cross, and our faith asks us to respond. If we are going to work in global mission at all, then we must try to find ways to remain with those communities that need us most, even under threat of violence.

On the other hand, it is foolish to risk death for no reason, and so the question then becomes: How can we witness to a God who accompanies us, and at the same time provide a presence that diminishes threats of violence and lays the groundwork for building a just peace? In this study I have attempted to outline a theology and praxis that would enable mis sionaries to stay.

This approach is based on the foundational principle of the dignity of each person, as created in God's image. Each of us has a right to life, and to all of the elements that allow life to flourish. A violation against one is a violation against God, and therefore against all of humanity.

One of those rights is to be the protagonist in one's own life story. The approach to mission outlined here rejects mission as a project of the mis sionary, who arrives with an agenda. The missionary agenda frequently falls into one of two categories: church-planting and coaxing individuals and communities to join the church; or fixing social problems through acts of charity. Church-planting risks repeating the mistakes of earlier waves of missionaries, who imposed their religion and destabilized an cient cultures. Acts of charity may cause the giver to feel good that he or she is doing something about poverty, but charity can also undermine human dignity by creating dependence on outside assistance.

In an accompaniment model the missionary arrives at the invitation of the receiving community with an agenda that they develop together. The missionary respects local culture and religious observances, but witnesses to her own faith in humility. The missionary accompanies the community and works to assist people in their own economic and human development projects. I suggest that this model applies not only to zones of violent conflict but to any mission context.

In a conflict zone, missionaries can become peacebuilders, providing a transformational presence that lowers the risk of violence and helps to facilitate reconciliation. International accompaniment in a zone of violent conflict, while risky, is a constructive, effective method for reducing the ef fects of war on unarmed populations. It also offers a powerful witness to a God who does not abandon those who suffer. Such a witness incorporates an active and public presence, living with the community but also partici pating in public actions, such as prayer and liturgy, which remember the victims, speak the truth, and proclaim the Gospel. This witness also re cords and reports violations to national and international authorities, and to constituencies overseas—especially the United States, Canada, and Eu rope, because these countries still have profound influence over what goes on in their former colonies. Finally, this witness stands with the people and provides assistance while they engage in dialogue with armed actors and with their own government, develop local democratic processes, train leadership, and initiate economic development.

There is much more work to be done. This investigation took place in one context with a specific kind of internal conflict. It would be useful, for example, to do a similar study in other zones of violent conflict to see whether the results match up. In some contexts, such as those that do not depend on the largesse of the government of the United States, accompaniment may not make sense. However, I am convinced that the model of international protective accompaniment developed here can contribute to building a just and lasting peace in many areas that have suffered from violent conflict and poverty for generations. My hope is that this work will contribute to engaging missionaries in reflecting on the spirituality and objectives of their mission work. I also hope that anyone who reads this will be inspired to both deepen their commitment to mission work and to conceive of it as part of a larger, global movement toward peace and justice for the world's most marginalized peoples. We must stop learning to live with atrocity.

Bibliography

Appleby, R. Scott. "The Many Dimensions of Catholic Peacebuilding." Paper presented at the 5th annual Catholic Peacebuilding Conference at Univeristy of Notre Dame, April 2008.

———. "Peacebuilding and Catholicism: Affinities, Convergences, Possibilities." In *Peacebuilding: Catholic Theology, Ethics, Praxis*, edited by Robert J. Screiter et al., 3–22. Maryknoll: Orbis, 2010.

Bevans, Stephen B. "From Edinburgh to Edinburgh: Toward a Missiology for a World Church." Scherer Lecture, Lutheran School of Theology at Chicago, February 2008.

———. "The Mission Has a Church: Responding to God's Call in Today's World." Unpublished Paper. March, 2009.

———. *Models of Contextual Theology*. Rev. ed. Maryknoll: Orbis, 2008.

———. "A Short History of Mission Today." Unpublished paper.

———. "Themes and Questions in Missiology Today." Unpublished paper.

Bevans, Stephen B., and Jeffrey Gros. *Evangelization and Religious Freedom*. New York: Paulist, 2009.

Bevans, Stephen B., and Roger P. Schroeder. *Constants in Context: A Theology of Mission for Today*. Maryknoll: Orbis, 2004.

———. *Prophetic Dialogue: Reflections on Christian Mission Today*. Maryknoll: Orbis, 2011.

Bosch, David. *Transforming Mission: Paradigm Shifts in Theology of Mission*. Maryknoll: Orbis, 1991.

Botman, H. Russel. "Narrative Challenges in a Situation of Transition." Chap. 4 in *To Remember and to Heal*, edited by H. Russel Botman and Robin M. Petersen. Cape Town: Human & Rousseau, 1996.

Bouvier, Virginia. "Building Peace in a Time of War." In *Colombia: Building Peace in a Time of War*, edited by Virginia Bouvier, 3–16. Washington, DC: United States Institute of Peace Press, 2009.

———. *Civil Society under Siege in Colombia*. United States Institute of Peace Special Report 114, February 2004.

———. *Harbingers of Hope: Peace Initiatives in Colombia*. United States Institute of Peace Special Report 169, August, 2006.

Cavanaugh, William T. *Torture and Eucharist: Theology, Politics, and the Body of Christ*. Oxford: Blackwell, 1998.

CELAM (Conferencia General del Episcopado Latinoamericano y del Caribe). *Documento de Aparecida*. Aparecida, May 13–31, 2007. http://www.celam.org/conferencia_aparecida.php.

Bibliography

Central Intelligence Agency. *The World Fact Book: Colombia.* https://www.cia.gov/library/publications/the-world-factbook/geos/co.html.

De Gruchy, John W. *Reconciliation: Restoring Justice.* Minneapolis: Fortress, 2002

ELCA. *Accompaniment: A Lens and Methodology for Mission Today.* Evangelical Lutheran Church in America, 2007.

————. *Global Mission in the 21st Century: A Vision of Evangelical Faithfulness in God's Mission.* Evangelical Lutheran Church in America, 1999.

Falla, Ricardo. *Masacres de la Selva: Ixcan, Guatemala (1975–1982).* Guatemala: Universidad de San Carlos de Guatemala, 1992.

Forero, Juan. "Colombia Orders Return of Stolen Farmland." *Washington Post*, March 23, 2009, A08.

————. "Unearthing Secrets of Colombia's Long War: Forensic Teams Track Victims 'Disappeared' by Death Squads." *Washington Post*, August 27, 2008, A06.

Franks, Jeff. "Colombia, FARC Rebels Reach Agreement on Agrarian Reform." *Reuters* May 27, 2013. http://www.reuters.com/article/2013/05/27/us-colombia-rebels-talks-idUSBRE94P0CA20130527.

Garay Salamanca, Lius Jorge, et al. *Impact of the US-Colombia FTA on the Small Farm Economy in Colombia.* Oxfam America, September 2009. http://www.oxfamamerica.org/files/colombia-fta-impact-on-small-farmers-final-english.pdf.

Garcia Duran, Mauricio. "Peace Mobilization in Colombia and the Role of the Roman Catholic Church: 1978-2006." Catholic Peacebuilding Network. http://cpn.nd.edu/conflicts-and-the-role-of-the-church/colombia/the-churchs-role-in-peacebuilding-in-colombia/peace-mobilization-in-colombia-and-the-role-of-the-roman-catholic-church-/.

Gittins, Anthony. "Beyond Liturgical Inculturation: Transforming the Deep Structures of Faith." *Irish Theological Quarterly* 69 (2004) 47–72.

Gonzalez, Fernan E. "The Colombian Conflict in Historical Perspective." *Accord* (2004) n.p. http://www.c-r.org/our-work/accord/colombia/historical-perspective.php.

Gonzalez, Justo. "Voices of Compassion." *Missiology: An International Review* 20 163–73.

Goodner, David. "Colombia's Bad Indians' Uprising: Meeting with Cauca Indigenous." *Colombia Reports*, August 22, 2008. http://colombiareports.com/opinion/human-rights/1742-colombias-bad-indians-uprising-meeting-with-cauca-indigenous.html.

Guroian, Vigen. "When Remembering Brings Redemption: Faith and the Armenian Genocide." In *The Spectre of Mass Death*, edited by David Power and Kabasele Lumbala, 77–88. Maryknoll: Orbis, 1993.

Gutierrez, Gustavo. *Las Casas: In Search of the Poor of Jesus Christ.* Maryknoll: Orbis, 1993.

Haugaard, Lisa, et al. *A Compass for Colombia Policy.* Washington, DC: Latin American Working Group Education Fund, 2008. http://www.usofficeoncolombia.org/docs/compass_for_colombia_policy.pdf.

Henao Gaviria, Hector Fabio. "The Colombian Church and Peacebuilding." In *Colombia: Building Peace in a Time of War*, edited by Virginia Bouvier, 173 Washington, DC: US Institute of Peace, 2009.

Human Rights Watch. "Summary and Recommendations." In *Breaking the Grip? Obstacles to Justice for Paramilitary Mafias in Colombia*, 3–19. Report. October 2008. http://www.hrw.org/sites/default/files/reports/colombia1008web.pdf.

———. *World Report 2013*. https://www.hrw.org/sites/default/files/wr2013_web.pdf.

John Paul II. *Redemptoris Missio*. Encyclical on the permanent validity of the Church's missionary mandate. Rome, December 7, 1990. http://www.vatican.va/holy_father/john_paul_ii/encyclicals/documents/hf_jp-ii_enc_07121990_redemptoris-missio_en.html.

Katz Garcia, Mauricio. "A Regional Peace Experience: The Magdalena Medio Peace and Development Programme." *Accord* 14 (2004) n.p. http://www.c-r.org/our-work/accord/colombia/regional-peace-experience.php.

Kern, Kathleen. *As Resident Aliens: Christian Peacemaker Teams in the West Bank 1995–2005*. Eugene, OR: Cascade, 2010.

———. *In Harm's Way: A History of Christian Peacemaker Teams*. Eugene, OR: Cascade, 2009.

Lamberty, Kim. "Mission as Prophetic Dialogue: A Case Study from Colombia." *Missiology: An International Review*, August 2, 2013. Published online ahead of print: http://mis.sagepub.com/content/early/2013/07/30/0091829613498186.abstract.

———. "Report: Conference on the Future of Catholic Peacebuilding." Unpublished Paper. University of Notre Dame, April 2008.

Lapsley, Michael. "Bearing the Pain in Our Bodies." Chap. 1 in *To Remember and To Heal*, edited by H. Russel Botman and Robin M. Petersen. Cape Town: Human & Rousseau, 1996.

Lari, Andrea. *Striving for Better Days: Improving the Lives of Internally Displaced People in Colombia*. Refugees International, December 2007.

Lederach, John Paul. "The Long Journey Back to Humanity: Catholic Peacebuilding with Armed Actors." In *Peacebuilding: Catholic Theology, Ethics, Praxis*, edited by Robert J. Screiter et al., 23–55. Maryknoll: Orbis, 2010.

———. *The Moral Imagination: The Art and Soul of Building Peace*. Oxford: Oxford University Press, 2005.

Library of Congress Federal Research Division. *Country Profile: Colombia*. February 2007. http://lcweb2.loc.gov/frd/cs/profiles/Colombia.pdf.

Loney, James. "From the Tomb." Christian Peacemaker Teams, April 19, 2006. Online: http://www.cpt.org/cptnet/2006/04/19/iraqtoronto-ampquotfrom-tombampquot-easter-reflection-james-loney.

Louf, André. *Grace Can Do More: Spiritual Accompaniment and Spiritual Growth*. Kalamazoo, MI: Cistercian, 2002.

Montville, Joseph V. "Justice and the Burdens of History." Chap. 7 in *Reconciliation, Justice, and Coexistence*, edited by Mohammed Abu-Nimer. Lanham, MD: Lexington, 2001.

Norby, Michael, and Brian Fitzpatrick. "The Horrific Costs of the US-Colombia Trade Agreement." *The Nation*, May 31, 2013. http://www.thenation.com/article/174589/horrific-costs-us-colombia-trade-agreement#.

Parroquia del Santísimo Cristo de Tiquisio y Programa de Desarrollo y Paz de Magdalena Medio. *Proceso Ciudadano por Tiquisio*. Report on the outcomes of the Tiquisio Citizens' Process. June 2008.

Bibliography

Paul VI. *Evangelii Nuntiandi*. Apostolic exhortation on evangelization in the modern world. Rome, December 8, 1975. http://www.vatican.va/holy_father/paul_vi/apost_exhortations/documents/hf_p-vi_exh_19751208_evangelii-nuntiandi_en.html.

———. *Populorum Progressio*. Encyclical on the development of peoples. Rome, March 26, 1967. http://www.vatican.va/holy_father/paul_vi/encyclicals/documents/hf_p-vi_enc_26031967_populorum_en.html.

Payne, William. "Colombia: Looking for the Prophets." Christian Peacemaker Teams, October 27, 2001. http://www.cpt.org/cptnet/2001/10/27/colombia-looking-prophets.

Romero, Simon. "Colombian Army Commander Resigns in Scandal Over Killing of Civilians." *New York Times*, November 4, 2008. http://www.nytimes.com/2008/11/05/world/americas/05colombia.html?scp=1&sq=Colombian%20Army%20commander%20Resigns%20Over%20Killing%20of%20Civilians&st=cse.

Schirch, Lisa. *Ritual and Symbol in Peacebuilding*. Bloomfield, CT: Kumarian, 2005

Schreiter, Robert J. "Challenges Today to Mission 'Ad Gentes.'" Paper delivered to the Meeting of the Superiors General of Societies of Apostolic Life, Maryknoll, NY, May 1, 2000.

———. "Changes in Roman Catholic Attitudes toward Proselytism and Mission." In *New Directions in Mission & Evangelization*, edited by James A. Scherer and Stephen B. Bevans, 2:113–25. Maryknoll: Orbis, 1994.

———. *The Ministry of Reconciliation: Spirituality and Strategies*. Maryknoll: Orbis, 1998.

———. *The New Catholicity: Theology between the Global and the Local*. Maryknoll: Orbis, 1997.

———. *Reconciliation: Mission and Ministry in Changing Social Order*. Maryknoll: Orbis, 1992.

Schreiter, Robert J., et al. *Peacebuilding: Catholic Theology, Ethics, and Praxis*. Maryknoll: Orbis, 2010.

Smedley, Audrey. *Race in North America: Origin and Evolution of a Worldview Edition*. Boulder: Westview, 2007.

Spring, Carol Foltz. "Colombia: Claimed Collaboration." Christian Peacemaker Teams, April 5, 2002. http://www.cpt.org/cptnet/2002/04/05/colombia-claimed-collaboration.

Suess, Paulo. *Evangelizar desde los proyectos históricos de los otros*. Quito: Abya-Yala, 1995.

US Office on Colombia. "Attacks on Human Rights Defenders on the Rise in February 18, 2013. http://www.usofficeoncolombia.org/.

———. *Body Counts & Injustice in Colombia's Armed Conflict*. Report. November http://www.usofficeoncolombia.org/uploads/application-pdf/2008-november%20eje%20report%20(final%20PDF).pdf.

Vatican Council II. *Ad Gentes*. Decree on the missionary activity of the Church. Promulgated by Pope Paul VI, December 7, 1965. http://www.vatican.va/archive/hist_councils/ii_vatican_council/documents/vat-ii_decree_19651207_ad_gentes_en.html.

Vidal, Hernán. *El Movimiento Contra la Tortura Sebastián Acevedo: Derechos Humanos y la Produccion de Simbolos Nacionales bajo el Fascismo Chileno*. Edina, MN:

Society for the Study of Contemporary Hispanic and Lusophone Revolutionary Cultures, 1986.

Volf, Miroslav. *Exclusion and Embrace: A Theological Exploration of Identity, Otherness and Reconciliation.* Nashville: Abingdon, 1996.

Wander, Philip C., et al. "The Roots of Racial Classification." In *White Privilege: Essential Readings on the Other Side of Racism*, edited by Paula S. Rothenberg, 29–34. 2nd ed. New York: Worth, 2005.

LIST OF INTERVIEWS

All interviews were recorded using a digital recorder.

Micoahumado

Ana F. Garay, member of the Morales Municipal Council, representing Micoahumado.

Fredy Caceres Sanchez, member of the Morales Municipal Council, representing Micoahumado.

Arisolina Rodriquez, social worker, leadership of the Constituent Assembly.

Doña Maria (last name withheld), community elder.

Eliadoro Virguez, leadership of Constituent Assembly, representing the vereda La Guasima.

Gladys Garita, leadership of Constituent Assembly, representing the vereda La Guasima.

Eugenio Gomez Quiñon, leadership of Constituent Assembly, representing the vereda La Caoa.

Juan Bautista Colorado, leadership of Constituent Assembly and of the Miners' Federation of the South of Bolivar (a labor union).

Julio Cesar Arbolera Hernandez, leadership of Constituent Assembly and Commission on Dialogue.

Victor Julio Gomez Sangaripa, shop owner.

Pablo de Jesus Santiago, leadership of Constituent Assembly.

Wilson Ropero, leadership of ASOPROMIC, in charge of coffee project.

Tiquisio

Delia Castro, leadership of the Tiquisio Citizens' Process, and of the Miners' Federation of the South of Bolivar (a labor union).

Ever Jesus Perez Vega, leadership of the Tiquisio Citizens' Process, representing the vereda Agua Fria.

Felix Villegas Fernandez, leadership of Tiquisio Citizens' Process.

Jorge Tafur, leadership of the Tiquisio Citizens' Process, and of the Miners' Federation of the South of Bolivar (a labor union).

Maria Ines de Hernandez Rodriguez, leader of the Madres Comunitarias and part of the Citizens' Process.

Miguel Cardenas, leadership of Tiquisio Citizens' Process, community elder.

Rafael Gallego, pastor of Parroquia Santisimo Cristo and leader of the Tiquisio Citizens' Process.

Programa de Desarrollo y Paz de Magdalena Medio

Francisco DeRoux, SJ, founder and director until 2008. Currently provincial of the Colombian Province of the Society of Jesus.
Ubencel Duque, associate director.

Christian Peacemaker Teams

Sandra Milena Rincon, coordinator, Colombia Team.

Made in the USA
Lexington, KY
03 November 2014